A Most Unlikely Story

A Short Memoir
of a Long Life

Emy Thomas

Cover by OffGridGraphics—Colleen Sullivan

AuthorHouse™
1663 Liberty Drive
Bloomington, IN 47403
www.authorhouse.com
Phone: 1 (800) 839-8640

Published by AuthorHouse 03/05/2020

ISBN: 978-1-7283-4760-8 (sc)
ISBN: 978-1-7283-4761-5 (e)

Library of Congress Control Number: 2020903243

Printed in the United States of America.

author HOUSE®

Also by Emy Thomas

Non-Fiction

Home Is Where the Boat Is
Life in the Left Lane

Acknowledgements

Thanks to Apple Gidley for multiple readings of the manuscript and much moral support.

Thanks to Deirdre Cooper for a comment that unknowingly would become my title.

Thanks to Diane Butler for her photography and tech support.

Thanks to Jan Buttler for proof-reading.

Special thanks to Colleen Sullivan for her inspired cover photo and design.

Contents

I
MY YOUTH
1933-1955

Introduction

I was born lucky—American, white and female with no apparent malfunctions. I had caring parents who made sure I got a good education. I had enough talent to have a nice short career in journalism. I had one great love, with whom I sailed half way around the world. I found my perfect home on a tropical island, had modest success as an author and artist, and have just enough time left to put that lucky life in book form. For a shy and quiet Connecticut WASP it's a most unlikely story

Washington, CT

I was born November 20, 1933 at the hospital in New Milford, CT. My parents lived nearby in another small town, Washington, CT, where my father taught at The Gunnery, a boarding school for boys. He left that job to help start Romford, another boys' school in Washington. The family lived on campus at both schools but I have no recollection of anything at that time.

I was named Maria Emilia Thomas, after the woman who raised my mother, but I've never been called anything but Emy.

East Hampton, Long Island, NY

In my first memory I am about 4, sitting on the floor of a big old house making a Christmas present for my mother. It's a necklace-- blue glass crescents and small white beads-- that was still in her jewelry box when she died 80-some years later. I liked making presents. Later I knit Argyle socks for my father year after year. There were always bits of yarn that unraveled, but he kindly wore them anyway, and I was very proud of my accomplishment.

We were living in East Hampton because my brother Tommy was going to Dr. Carlson's School for children with cerebral palsy. My father was teaching at a private school nearby. His sister Mary was taking care of Tommy and me while my mother was in the hospital with what was then called a "nervous breakdown". (I was never aware of more such incidents, though all her life she was emotionally fragile and had to be handled with care.)

The famous hurricane of 1938 struck and the roads were covered with fallen trees. Tommy had to stay at his school overnight and later I heard how distressed our parents were about not being able to bring him home. They had promised he would come home every day. He was 6.

In the winter Dr. Carlson's school moved to Pompano, Florida, and Mum and I went too. We lived in a tiny house. I went to Tommy's school once and was horrified/terrified by the kids, who were much worse off than Tommy. Most of them were not ambulatory and they had almost no control over their muscles.

A huge fire down the street one night petrified me. I don't think any buildings were burned, probably just vegetation, but in my mind it was monumental. Fires played a major role in my first memories. The "forest fire" in Pompano and later a small fire in the family car traumatized me.

We owned a gray Plymouth coupe. I was in the back seat when embers from Daddy's cigarette started a fire in the upholstery next to me. I was so frightened I would not ride in the back seat of that car ever again and I reacted fearfully to any flames-- even in a fireplace, even on a match lighting a cigarette-- for years.

(Oddly, as a young teenager, I did an about-face and became an amateur pyromaniac. A friend lived next to a golf course and more than once we set fire to the long grass bordering the fairway, then ran back to her house and watched the fire engines arrive. I don't think we felt any guilt. I think we felt a small thrill of power.)

My parents, my brother and me in the early 1930s.

Marion, Massachusetts

We moved from Long Island to Marion, Massachusetts, where Daddy taught at Tabor Academy, a boarding school for boys, for a few years. We lived in an old house on a highway out of town.

I don't remember nursery school or kindergarten but a report card my mother saved made me sound like someone I don't know—an independent little chatterbox who was quite charming. What happened to that little girl who sounds so comfortable and confident? I became quiet and timid and shy. I did retain an independent spirit but rarely acted on it until I was much older.

Daddy helped me learn to ride a bike on the side of the highway. I was afraid of the wobbly thing and once I fell off, skinning my knees. I got a lot of sympathy and attention, which I loved, and the injuries were bad enough that my parents gave up an evening out to stay home with me. That made me feel very special, and I repeated the incident at least once, accidentally I'm sure, a few years later when I came home bloody from another bike fall, this one requiring stitches by the pediatrician who was summoned for a house call. Again my parents were all dressed up for dinner out but stayed home with me. I felt really important, and loved. There was always a maid or baby sitter to be with us, and we loved most of them, but even so I apparently hated to have my parents leave me.

Me in Marion

Tommy (Philip H. Thomas Jr., whose nickname morphed to Tom when he was older) is two years older than I but, because of his cerebral palsy, caused by a forceps delivery at birth, he needed much more attention than I. My mother told the story on herself that it took a total stranger to point out to her that even though I wasn't as needy physically she should give me equal time.

I attended first and second grades in Marion, traveling by school bus into town. But dancing classes (ballet and tap) were the most important part of my life and dancing recitals were the major events.

My recital costumes included a peach-colored tutu and a red satin military coat with gold epaulettes and a matching hat. Mum must have made the costumes. She made school clothes for me too, an ability she stopped exercising soon after. I loved tap dancing. I practiced in the kitchen, disrupting preparations for dinner.

My father bought a piano for me and I reluctantly took lessons. It was an ugly old upright piano that cost $15 I think, a significant investment for our family then, and even though I must have shown absolutely no aptitude, the piano moved with us twice and I continued to take lessons until I was at least 12. Every year I suffered through a recital, terribly nervous that I would forget the music or have to scratch.

I was a problem eater. I wouldn't touch vegetables and Mum insisted I have spinach, I think every day. I remember going for my nap with spinach in my mouth, presumably because I wouldn't be excused from the table until it was off my plate.

The only food I enjoyed was dessert, especially chocolate pudding. (I'm still a chocoholic.) Once when I was sick a doctor diagnosed me as diabetic, but when he took me off chocolate pudding and gave me another blood test, my sugar was normal. (I've had similar occurrences as an adult.)

In Marion I had one inseparable friend, Elizabeth, who was pint-sized like me. Summers we spent all day at the public beach on the beautiful large harbor that is now a haven for yachts.

It was a small beach with a pier and not too far off-shore a raft with a high diving platform and a slide. I was afraid to dive off the high platform, but I loved the slide and remember wearing out the seat of at least one bathing suit.

We took swimming lessons and junior life saving classes. I was terrified of the deep dive off the pier required in the life saving test. It was probably only 6 feet or so but I was afraid I wouldn't be able to hold my breath long enough to get down, pick up the rock and return to the surface.

Elizabeth was in my dancing classes too. For recitals and other special occasions our mothers set our hair in rag curlers. Old sheets, always white, were torn into strips about 8 inches by 1, which were tied around locks of hair, rolled up and knotted again. When they were removed a few hours later we were as curly haired as Shirley Temple.

Daddy taught at Tabor about three years, then returned each summer for a few more years to teach summer school. The summer of VJ Day (1945) we lived in the town of Marion and celebrated in the streets with the rest of the townies with bonfires and fireworks.

That was the summer I "ran away from home," for some imagined slight. I got about a block away when I saw a friend and stopped to chat, then forgot about my intention and returned home. I don't recall ever trying again.

My Parents

My mother, "Kitty," was born Catherine McGeary in 1905 and died in 1995 at the age of 90. When she was 87 and knew her memory was failing, she wrote a short memoir (with a little help from me) which included an amazing number of facts, including her parents' names (Mary Veronica Duffy McGeary and Martin Thomas McGeary) and when they were born and died and their parents names and whether they were born in Ireland (the Duffys) or America (the McGearys, in Boston).

Tom remembers hearing that her father had been a motorman on the city's trolley cars. Her mother did some kind of domestic work.

Both her parents died in 1912 in New York City, she from double pneumonia and he two months later from tuberculosis. Their children, Kitty and Mary, were 8 and 10.

Kitty's sweet little memoir includes a story we offspring heard often. The McGeary family presumably lived somewhere in the vicinity of Third Avenue and 2nd St. in New York City, because that's where the girls went to Public School #27.

Directly across the street from the school was St. Bartholomew's Girls' Club, which their mother had always wished they could attend after school. Apparently the five cent enrollment fee for each girl was more than she could afford, but one day in 1911 she picked up a handkerchief on the sidewalk outside the girls' club and found a dime wrapped inside. She immediately walked in and enrolled both girls.

My mother's memoir recalls "the whole new world" of dancing, gymnastics, cooking, making paper flowers and acting in the play Alice in Wonderland. She was especially fond of her sewing teacher, and making sheets and pillow cases for a doll's bed.

That Christmas the sewing teacher brought presents of doll's furniture for each student. Uh-oh. There was one extra girl that day so she was short one present. Kitty offered her present to the extra girl and was rewarded with a trip to Macy's to pick out whatever she wanted. The teacher's liveried chauffeur drove them in her black limousine. Kitty chose "a little stove with burners that actually boiled water."

That little episode determined the path for the rest of her life.

The sewing teacher was Maria Emilia (Emy) Engelhard, wife of Charles W. Engelhard, both German immigrants. He made a fortune in precious metals and founded Engelhard Corporation in Newark, NJ. They lived in Bernardsville, NJ. (More on them in a separate section.)

The Engelhards never adopted Kitty and Mary, but their Bernardsville estate, Craigmore, eventually became their home.

The girls' legal guardian was Charlotte Boyd, director of the Girls' Club. She was an Episcopal deaconess, the equivalent of a Catholic nun. After the girls' mother died, their father, who had been in Seton Memorial Hospital for a long time and knew he was dying from TB, asked Miss Boyd to be the legal guardian of his girls. She agreed, despite the fact that the McGearys were Catholics.

Kitty and Mary first spent a few happy years on a farm for girls from broken homes in New York State. When they reached high school age, they moved to Craigmore.

They attended St. Agnes boarding school in Albany, N.Y. Mary went on to nursing school and married George Seel shortly after. Their daughter, Cathy, was a great older cousin to me and when I was still quite young—maybe 10—I was a bridesmaid in her wedding, her first of five. Uncle George was a foreman at one of the Engelhard factories.

Kitty went on to Wellesley College for a BA in German and MA in English. She then taught one year at Wyckham Rise, a girls' boarding school in Washington, CT, where she met Philip H. Thomas, who was teaching in the same town at a boys' boarding school, The Gunnery.

They were married at Craigmore in June, 1928. Tommy was born in 1931 and I in 1933. I inherited Aunt Emy's whole name, Maria Emilia, but luckily only the nickname stuck.

My father had worked his way through Yale and later did graduate work at Columbia. He remained a private school teacher all his short life. He died at 52.

The big depression apparently didn't impact us very much because my father's jobs at boarding schools included room and board for the whole family, first at The Gunnery and later at Romford, in the same town.

The Thomas side of the family had arrived in this country in the 1600s. They were Welsh and English. Tommy and I knew only one grandparent, my father's father, Elmer E. Thomas. He was a lawyer and a judge who lived in Omaha, Nebraska, where my father and his four siblings had grown up. Their mother died quite young.

The most interesting thing we ever heard about our grandfather involved a court case during Prohibition. The judge's ruling upset someone enough to toss a "bomb" onto grandad's porch. No one was hurt and the damage was slight, but it made a great story.

I think all their offspring went east for college. Two returned to Omaha—John, a doctor, and Lyman, who had an advertising business. My Uncle Elmer II was a lawyer who spent most of his career working for Engelhard Industries in New Jersey. Aunt Mary was a librarian in Tarrytown, NY.

The siblings had a total of 11 children so we had plenty of Thomas cousins. We got to know the relatives who lived in the east and Lyman's daughter Mary Marlin once she came east for college but we hardly knew the western part of the Thomas family. Once our generation was grown and had their own children, Thomas family reunions were held on the New Jersey shore for several summers. I was living in Puerto Rico then so attended only one.

I remember seeing my grandfather only once, when he visited us in Connecticut. Tom and I would have been about 10 and 8 then. I remember him as a kindly white-haired gentleman who started each day with a glass of lemon juice and always remembered our birthdays.

Tom's memory of him includes "a spiritual healing" for a wart cluster on his hand. Grandad sat beside him reading from a worn Bible and within days all the warts disappeared, never to return. Tom learned later from our father's diaries that Grandad had been a follower of Billy Sunday, the tent evangelist. He died soon after that visit.

My parents, Philip H. Thomas and Catherine McGeary Thomas

New Britain, Connecticut

We moved to New Britain, Connecticut, in 1941, when Daddy became headmaster of Mooreland Hill School, a private country day school for grades 7 through 9, then known as junior high school. He was there until his death in 1949.

New Britain was an industrial town known as "The Hardware City of the World."

Stanley Works and Fafnir Bearing were among the major factories there. Mooreland served the small population of executives' and professionals' children.

We rented a beautiful big 18th century house on the corner of Shuttle Meadow Avenue and Corbin Avenue. I had a big bedroom upstairs in the back of the house, where I remember daddy's rough back rubs putting me to sleep much better than Mum's soft ones. And I remember playing stewardess and bride in that room with my friend Polly.

Tommy and our parents had the two bedrooms in the front of the house. Our maid Bernice had a small room under the eaves. There was only one bathroom in that big house, at the top of the stairs.

Our telephone number was 686.

It now seems strange that a poor teacher's family had a live-in maid but at the time it was fairly common. They probably made very little money but they earned room and board and were often treated almost like members of the family.

Bernice was very pretty and we kids loved her. She had worked for us in Marion, where her family lived, and when we moved to New Britain she came with us. She acquired a boyfriend there and Mum was livid when she found them necking in the living room. She thought public displays of affection were disgusting. (But did Bernice ever have a night off so that she could see him privately?)

After she left to get married, Bernice sent Christmas cards with pictures of her family, including twins, but I suspect my mother never attempted to see her again.

Downstairs there was a parlor and dining room flanking the central entry hall, a small room behind the parlor where my piano loomed large, and a big kitchen. We had a large yard with big trees and a marvelous Concord grape arbor and a dilapidated barn, which we kids used as a meeting place for various "clubs".

There was a steep concrete driveway on one side of the house which my friends and I used for roller skating. I was afraid of the fast reckless descent but did it because my friends did, afraid to show that I was afraid.

During my youth I was often afraid. Whether it was roller skating or riding a roller-coaster or stealing from the 5&10, all of which terrified me, I was even more afraid to admit my weakness so did many things in absolute terror.

The roller-coaster was a turning point. I had bought my ticket along with the rest of the kids and stood in line with my heart pounding but at the last minute I turned away. I just couldn't get on. I was mortified that I had shown my fear but that episode helped me over a hurdle. I had admitted fear but it wasn't a big deal. I wasn't ostracized.

Our house was just two blocks away from Vance School, where I went for grades 3 through 6. I have few recollections of it. I loved the teacher I had in 3rd and 4th grades. I wanted my parents to adopt a classmate who lived at the orphanage nearby. I was fascinated that she wore the same dress every day and that it always looked clean and freshly ironed.

I had two inseparable friends, Ann and Polly, who came to my house after school almost every day. Our snack was peanut butter and marshmallow fluff, not in a sandwich but by the tablespoonful, scooped out of gallon-size jars.

Ann's father had died. Her mother had an important job at the local hospital, the only mother I knew who worked (well, mine did too but only as an infrequent substitute teacher). Her grandmother, a big Red Sox fan, lived with them and helped raise Ann and two older brothers.

Polly's family lived a block away and I envied their home life, which was warm and affectionate. She had an older brother and a younger sister. Her parents actually cuddled together while we all listened to Jack Benny and Fred Allen on the radio Sunday nights. My parents never showed affection to each other or to us.

I needed more affection than I got. I also needed more attention than I got. Not knowing how to ask for it, I would go all moody until my mother asked what was wrong. Only then did I feel I could tell her what was on my mind.

(I still find it hard to come right out and talk about myself, whether I've had a tragedy or a triumph. As an author, I'm hopeless at promoting my own books; I'm unable to insert them into a conversation. Even if I'm bursting with news I usually keep it to myself unless I'm given an opening. Someone just has to say What's up? Then I feel entitled to tell.)

I spent every afternoon in bed one school year, doctor's orders. Apparently he considered me dangerously underweight and thought I would fatten up if I wasn't outside running around. I don't think it worked.

I was 8 when the U.S. entered World War II.

Apparently our government seriously considered the east coast a probable target by air as well as sea. We all were required to prepare for an aerial attack at night, with black shades in all the windows so that no lights could be seen from above and frequent air-raid drills. Daddy was an air-raid warden. Every time the terrifying siren sounded the alarm Daddy left the house wearing a helmet to patrol the darkened streets. Mum, Tommy and I sat at the kitchen table with a small lamp playing games. Mum volunteered as a plane spotter during the day.

We must have seen newsreels about the war, because I had very graphic images of the Germans in my head and nightmares about them coming to get me. Our old colonial house had big fireplaces, one with a Dutch oven. I was small enough that I planned to hide in there when the Germans came.

There was a large flower garden in the yard. I was paid a quarter an hour to weed it. I could also earn pennies, one for each fly I killed.

There was a bottling factory in an old barn across the street where we all bought sodas. I think my friends and I stole more than we paid for, just helping ourselves from the refrigerator inside the door when no one was around. I drank birch beer, root beer, pepsi cola, orange soda and cream soda.

One friend took me on more serious stealing expeditions. We took the bus downtown after school and went to the Kresge 5&10 Cent Store and there we shoplifted small items of jewelry and clothes. I was scared to death of being caught. We never were. I was such a victim of peer pressure I found it easier to steal than admit that I was afraid. We took all the loot to my friend's house and I'm amazed that her parents never noticed or never did anything about it.

Summers we usually returned to Marion where Daddy taught summer school at Tabor, but one year he had a summer job at a boy's tutorial camp in Maine so I was put in a girl's camp in New Hampshire. I was terribly homesick, but I learned to ride horseback and play tennis and I was good at diving. I was about 10.

We all walked or rode bikes when we were kids. Our parents never drove us anywhere except to dancing school, when we were all dressed up and came home after dark.

After school we usually hung out at each other's houses and played games or joined in a baseball game at a makeshift diamond on a vacant lot.

This was in the 1940s and our parents never seemed to worry about us. We were free to come and go. They often had no idea where we were but we all knew we had to be home by dark.

I feel so sorry for the kids today who have their "free" time completely programmed and are driven everywhere and must be in constant cell phone contact with their parents. I'm glad I grew up in a more innocent and free era.

At dancing school, I and my friends learned ballroom dancing, the waltz and foxtrot, in the re-purposed basement of the teacher's elegant home. At that elementary school age, most of the girls were taller than most of the boys. I was a pipsqueak so was always paired with the short boys, who always seemed to be the nerdy ones.

We dressed up for dancing classes and wore white socks with black patent leather Mary Jane shoes. I don't remember whether we wore white gloves but it's quite likely. We certainly had to wear them to church and when traveling. A hat and gloves were de rigeur for all ladies and little girls in the 40s and 50s.

I started Sunday School at a Congregational church. Mum had been raised an Episcopalian and Daddy a Presbyterian. I hated Sunday School because my teacher insisted on calling me Eemy. She knew for a fact that when spelled with one M the name should not be pronounced as in Emmy.

I requested changing to the Episcopal church, because that's where Ann and Polly went, and my wish was granted. I was confirmed at St. Mark's Church when I was 13, I think, though I wonder if I comprehended any of the catechism I studied. I certainly didn't retain anything. I don't remember going to church after that until I was at prep school, where attendance at chapel was required.

I lost my virginity to a bicycle when I was about 10, although it was years before I realized what had happened. I don't know why I was riding a boy's bike but I slipped off the seat onto the bar. It was painful and I bled. I never confided the incident to my mother, and if she knew about it she never mentioned it. She certainly didn't explain about the hymen. Now it seems strange to me that neither of us brought up the subject. Today it seems that mothers and daughters share every little hiccup. I don't know whether our relationship was typical of the times or unique for us.

After renting our wonderful house for five years, we had to move out. The owners decided to sell it and we couldn't afford the $3,000 to buy it. We rented a couple of other houses in the next couple of years. I liked the brick one on Lincoln Street because it was modern but did not like the one on Vine Street. It was a two or three-family house and I considered that very lower class.

On Vine Street I started to be interested in boys. I liked one who conveniently lived on the same street. Our dancing teacher held "recitals" every year at the Shuttle Meadow Country Club. I had a "date" with my neighbor Dick and wore my first long gown, a hand-me-down from cousin Mary, a pink confection. His father, our family doctor, drove us to the dance.

Unlike most of my friends, I rarely did baby-sitting. I never felt comfortable with young kids, especially babies.

And unlike most of my friends I never experienced a joyful Christmas. We always went to New Jersey to be with the Engelhards.

The Engelhards

I've always envied my friends whose lives were enhanced by loving grand-parents. The Engelhards did not fill that grand-parental niche for us although they were a big part of our family's life. Our frequent visits to their Bernardsville home—every Christmas and other occasions—felt more like punishment than pleasure for Tom and me (and I suspect for my father also).

Aunt Emy and Uncle Charles had immigrated to the U.S. in the early 20th century. By the time my mother knew them, Uncle Charles had made a fortune in the precious metals field. According to Wikipedia, in 1905 his consolidated companies "became the world's largest refiner and fabricator of platinum metals, gold and silver, a producer of silver and silver alloys in mill forms, operator of the world's largest precious metals smelter."

Aunt Emy and Uncle Charles led very sedate, formal lives, with strict schedules. We had to greet Uncle Charles at the door every evening when he returned from work with "Good evening, Uncle Charles."

My mother and her sister had been taught to call their benefactors aunt and uncle, and when their husbands and children came along, we were all told to do the same.

Meals were in an enormous dining room full of dark, heavy claw foot furniture, where maids served each of us and conversation was forced. My mother would rehearse us with questions we might be asked and answers we should give.

Christmas was a far cry from the joyful, boisterous extravaganzas our friends experienced. Ours was European style, celebrated Christmas Eve with a feast followed by gift giving in the loggia, where a huge Christmas tree reached the high ceiling. I remember blue and silver decorations.

Every person there sat quietly in a chair and presents were opened carefully one by one. As the gift was displayed around the room, the recipient rose from his/her chair to shake hands with the donor and thank him/her for the gift, then return to his seat. For shy little me, going through this performance was pure torture.

My gift from the Engelhards every year was a doll—a very special doll from one European country or another, who came complete with her own trunk full of an ethnically appropriate wardrobe. Unfortunately I did not appreciate them at all—neither the craftsmanship nor their playability as toys. I preferred stuffed animals, something soft that I could cuddle.

Of course the Engelhards couldn't know that so I continued to receive these exquisite gifts every year and ended up with quite a collection that gathered dust in the attic. I never thought to do something constructive with this collection, like give it to a museum or sell it. Instead I gave it away.

The best part of any Bernardsville visit for Tom and me was a visit to the farm at the bottom of the hill and the man who ran it, Henry. He was the only person on the estate we felt comfortable with. We were able to be normal kids with him; we could play anywhere on the farm.

A stable housing huge Arabian horses was the main feature of that farm. Their only purpose seemed to be to provide Uncle Charles with a brisk daily ride. I seem to remember three of these valuable steeds.

First thing every morning Henry rode up the long and curvy gravel driveway to the mansion's front door with two horses. He helped portly Uncle Charles mount one from a step-stool, then he nimbly boarded the other and they were off into trails in the woods. They returned in time for Uncle Charles to dress, have breakfast and enter his chauffeur-driven car for the short ride to the train station, where he boarded his private club car on the commuter train that would carry him to his business.

The farm served other purposes too. There were enough cows to produce enough milk for Henry to have a small delivery business. He offered to take us with him one morning and we sneaked out very early. Riding in the bed of the pick-up with all the milk bottles was the most fun thing we ever did in Bernardsville. Unfortunately for us and for Henry, someone spotted us there on our return and we were all punished for the "dangerous" infraction.

The Engelhards were childless when they took in the two McGeary girls, but Charles W. Engelhard Jr. was born a couple of years later, in 1917. Charlie inherited the family business after his father died in 1950. He expanded it into South Africa, where the mines are.

Unlike his reserved parents, he made quite a splash, marrying an elegant socialite, Jane Mannheimer, raising five daughters (one is now Mrs. Oscar de la Renta), owning race horses (Nijinski is the most famous), running unsuccessfully—as a Democrat-- for state senate, and founding the philanthropic Charles Engelhard Foundation, which still supports numerous organizations from education and medical research to wildlife and conservation. With his gold mine connections in South Africa, he was thought by many to be the inspiration for Ian Fleming's film "Goldfinger."

When we were still going to Bernardsville for holidays we now had the added attraction of this fascinating young family living on their own grand estate nearby.

Charlie died in 1971 at the age of 54. His widow Jane carried on his philanthropy and expanded it. Her most stunning gift: The Charles Engelhard Court in the American Wing of the Metropolitan Museum of Art in New York City, a vast sky-lit pavilion filled with fabulous art.

Jane Engelhard

Charles W. Engelhard Jr.

Our family visits became less frequent when Tom and I were in our teens. Mum continued to visit Aunt Emy in Bernardsville and New York City, where Aunt Emy had first a suite at the Plaza Hotel and later an apartment in Waldorf Towers. Mum also served all her life as a travel companion to the Engelhards, who often visited spas and other vacation spots in Europe and the States. Mum continued to go whenever and wherever summoned.

Once when I was with Mum and Aunt Emy at the Plaza I saw that the Benny Goodman band was playing at the night club there. I was too young to go alone and of course Aunt Emy had no interest in it but my dear mother offered to accompany me. The maître d' squeezed us into the packed room and brought us complimentary drinks and I was in heaven for the next couple of hours hearing my favorite clarinetist, Benny Goodman, The King of Swing, and his big band.

In all the years of this relationship, the Engelhards never visited us. I'm sure they were never invited. Mum must have reasoned that she couldn't duplicate their lifestyle and they could never adjust to ours. She must have felt quite schizophrenic, alternating between our simple home where she was cook and bottle washer and their elaborate spread where she was waited on by several servants and had her own suite!

Some of Mum's friends talked her into inviting Aunt Emy for a visit. They had heard so much about her they wanted to see her in person. They promised to help entertain her and they did, with tea parties and bridge games.

She stayed in a hotel and was there for only a few days but Mum prepared the house as for a state visit. I'm glad I was away at school or college when this happened but I heard about the frantic cleaning and redecorating and the elaborate scheduling of events so that every meal and every moment was carefully planned.

Aunt Emy was apparently delighted with the visit. She must have been curious all those years about Mum's life and glad to finally see what it was all about.

The memoir that my mother wrote toward the end of her life was intended as a thank you to the Engelhard family, whose generosity to our family lives on today.

Tom and I were given shares in Engelhard stocks when we were very young. We had our own savings accounts as soon as we were old enough and deposited our quarterly checks religiously. They didn't amount to a whole lot in the beginning but they kept growing.

I know the Engelhards also made it possible for me to have an excellent education. I earned partial scholarships to prep school and college but they paid the rest.

My mother had, of course, been receiving dividends from Engelhard stock all along, helping our family survive. After she was widowed for the second time, in 1966, Charlie really stepped up, creating a very generous trust fund for her.

He must have increased our income too because I know that by the time I "dropped out" and went sailing in 1972, I had such a nice bank account I didn't have to earn a cent. That lasted for 13 years—a time of very few expenses to be sure—and when I then decided to build a house I still had enough to cover those costs! And when my mother died 10 years later she still had enough to leave Tom and me financially comfortable for the rest of our lives.

We have lost all touch with the Engelhard family. Jane died in 2004 and there has been no further contact. I wasn't sure if Kitty's memoir/thank you had ever been sent to any of them so after her death I wrote my own thank you to the daughters and sent those with copies of the memoir to the last address I could find for each. I got no replies. I hope they know what a huge contribution their family made to ours, and how much we appreciate it.

Aunt Emy with large lap dog and my mother

A Farm in Southington, Connecticut

The summer after I finished elementary school we moved to Southington, then a rural town adjacent to New Britain. We moved into another old colonial house on a corner with about 15 acres of land, mostly wooded. It needed a lot of work and must have been dirt cheap because we actually bought it.

Daddy's dream was to have a farm. In addition to making the house habitable he planted a huge vegetable garden. This was a man with a heart condition and a job as headmaster of a country day school. The long summer vacations were busy.

The house was Cape Cod style, circa 1790. It had a central chimney with fireplaces in three rooms-- the parlor and dining room flanking the central entrance, and what became the living room in the back of the house after Daddy put in a floor. There was some kind of structure behind the bathroom, which became the master bedroom, and behind that Daddy built a patio with big fieldstones from the property.

Upstairs in the attic Tommy and I each had a bedroom under the eaves, along with hornets' nests. My room was big and sunny. Tommy's was small and dark. I decorated mine with posters of movie stars. I liked tough guys, the cruder the better, much to my mother's distress. I see Victor Mature with sensuous lips, sneering.

We lived there the three years I went to my father's school, Mooreland. Then his health was so precarious the doctor ordered us back to town. Daddy had had rheumatic fever as a teenager, which left him with a rheumatic heart. Maybe he knew the farm would kill him, and maybe he thought it was worth it. He loved working in his garden, plowing with his roto-tiller, planting and picking, looking up at the surrounding hills to rest.

We had all kinds of vegetables, most famously cucumbers and corn. We ate cucumbers like bananas and put away multiple ears of corn at every dinner in season. Daddy and Tommy were both big eaters (though lean) and competed over corn consumed—up to a dozen ears at a sitting.

Our parents set Tommy up in the chicken business, buying him 100 chicks which he kept in a dilapidated shed on the property. My job was to sell vegetables and eggs from a table on the side of the road. Now I can't think of a better occupation but then I was mortified, afraid that friends from town would venture out into the country and see me at my bumpkin work.

I was 11 to 13 those country years, just the wrong age to appreciate the farm. I resented being unable to hang out with the rest of the kids after school, listening to Frank Sinatra records at a friend's house. He crooned, we swooned.

But I fantasized that a Hollywood scout might pass by my stand and discover me. Really! I was a skinny, scrawny kid but apparently I had a good self-image then. I think I got to keep any money I made on vegetables but I probably had to share egg money with Tom.

The summer I was 13 I fell in love with Johnny. He was the son of Sue, Mum's college roommate who had remained a close friend. A divorcee, she and Johnny lived in an apartment in Manhattan and they were the most glamorous people I knew. Johnny spent a summer, or at least a good part of one, with us on the farm. He was handsome and sophisticated, with more than one girlfriend sending him frequent letters while he was there.

I had always adored him and was swept away when I became the object of his attention, even though I knew that I wasn't really chosen, that I was simply the only girl in sight. I had never even been kissed before. I was thrilled by the attention and the idea of having a boyfriend.

I'm sorry to say my mother quickly made me feel that it was wrong. When she saw Johnny and me holding hands, she angrily informed me that I should never show affection in public.

When Johnny's visit was over I was bereft. I saw him occasionally in the next few years when we went to football games at his prep school or our families visited each other, but we were never intimate again. The summer before we entered college I realized I might never see him again. He was going west to college and talking about joining the Marines. I don't remember ever feeling quite so brokenhearted ever again and, although I went on to other boyfriends and eventually lovers and rarely thought about him, he retained an important place in my heart until I finally saw him again about forty years later. He was a fine and fun person and I enjoyed being with him but hooray! I wasn't in love! A great burden was lifted but I felt really stupid having carried a torch so long for the memory of a boy.

We grew many more vegetables than we could eat or sell, so we froze the rest. This was a family project, all of us in the kitchen blanching green beans, peas, squash, etc., well into the night, then packing them into small boxes, then quickly driving into town where we rented a freezer locker. Eventually we bought a home freezer we put in the basement. I think they were quite a new thing then, and I wonder how we afforded it.

The basement had a dirt floor and was unheated. We used it as a root cellar for the potatoes, onions and other root vegetables we grew.

In retrospect it's hard to picture my mother participating in the freezing process or any other farm-wife chore. Until then she had always had a maid. She definitely saw herself as a lady.

We had a Welsh Terrier, Billy, who had been in the family as long as I could remember. He and Tommy had a classic boy-and-his-dog relationship. Billy chased cars and was eventually killed by one. We were all devastated, more for Tommy I think than for the dog.

A while later we acquired a Border Collie from a friend who raised them. Presumably the idea was to replace Billy in Tommy's life but they never really bonded and Tess was more my dog than his.

One summer Tommy and some of his friends found a box holding a litter of newborn kittens by the side of a brook. They brought it home and the kittens were distributed around the neighborhood.

We kept one that I adored. She never grew much. We called her Midge. Tess mothered Midge and slept wrapped around her, with Midge nestled against her stomach. Tess carried Midge around in her mouth and flung her around playfully. One day she must have flung her too hard and too far. We never saw her again.

I was still taking piano lessons. I now had to ride my bike a few miles to the piano teacher's house. One day a dog nipped me on the leg and I thought now I can stop, but no. It wasn't much of a bite, not enough to stop riding.

I wonder why my parents were so persistent about my piano lessons. I'm sure I was never any good and as soon as they were over I never played again and I forgot everything I learned. I can't read music now.

I was able to ride horseback at a farm down the road and eventually was allowed to ride alone on the neighbor's horse, Scotty, a small, multi-colored spotty animal who never scared me as some of the other horses did (though I couldn't admit that).

Many of the roads nearby were unpaved and I scouted out a route from home to school almost entirely on dirt roads. I dreamed of buying Scotty and riding the few miles to Mooreland every day rather than riding in the car with my father. The farmer who owned him said he would sell him for $100. I had $100 in savings bonds and told my parents of my plan. I was crushed when they pointed out we had nowhere to keep a horse and that I would need a lot more money to feed him.

My Brother

Philip H. Thomas Jr., who was called Tommy when young, Tom as he grew older, is my favorite person in all the world.

He was born with cerebral palsy, the result of a brain injury at birth, in his case a forceps delivery. As he grew it became apparent that he couldn't walk and talk like other children.

Once he was diagnosed, my parents did everything they knew of to help him. In toddler-age photos he has braces on his legs. When he was 5 he started attending institutions for crippled children, which concentrated on walking and speech therapies.

In a terrific essay he wrote recently, Tom said that up until then, despite all the attention he got for his "spastic motor skills, slurred speech and excessive drooling", he had never thought of himself as different. Being thrown in with children with terrible disabilities was a nightmare for him.

Mum continued the therapies at home and as he got older he resented that, seeing no "payoff" and wanting to be out playing with his friends. As Tom points out in his essay, "during this "fix Tom era", all attention was on his physical defects. "My fear, anxiety, resentments and anger were not acknowledged as normal but as added defects.""

He rebelled, and from then on he bounced from school to school, his behavior always a problem. He didn't even last long at the school where Daddy was headmaster. But he finally did make it through high school and even made a brief try at the University of Connecticut.

Then he left home to be on his own and started supporting himself financially, doing odd jobs in Florida and New Jersey and writing a little. He came back to New Britain for another job and soon met Joan Gavitt, who soon became his wife.

Joan also has cerebral palsy; she is less physically handicapped than Tom but has a worse speech defect and is deaf but, like Tom, was determined to live a "normal" life. She was working in an insurance office when they met.

Tom started his own business as a milkman. Milk was still sold in glass bottles in the 50s and delivered to back doors by the milkman. Tom arose in the middle of the night, drove to a nearby dairy where he loaded his truck with crates of milk bottles, then drove all over town delivering to his ever-increasing list of customers. He had a great reputation for punctuality and reliability. Neither snow nor sleet kept him from his appointed rounds.

When dairies started selling their milk in plastic containers, in stores and supermarkets, milkmen were out of business so Tom became a deliveryman for a bakery, supplying super markets and smaller shops with their bread and cakes.

He also did a brief stint as a door-to-door salesman for Fuller Brush.

Then he got a terrific job working for the state as a driver for the Department of the Blind, driving a blind woman all over the state to the blind clients she helped to cope with living alone. He did that until he retired with a nice pension and excellent health insurance.

Meanwhile he and Joan had three sons-- Philip III, Robert and John. They all inherited practical skills from Joan's side of the family. Each can build a house and fix anything. John is an engineer—and a sailor. I like to think I launched him when he learned to sail my dinghy in the British Virgin Islands.

They now all have children of their own—a total of seven. And there are already four in the next generation.

"The boys", Tom's sons, all live nearby and play a big part in keeping their parents in their own home. Both well into their 80s, Tom and Joan need assistance and the boys make sure they get it.

Tom has done a lot of writing in his retirement years. Well after his education rebellion he took a number of writing courses at nearby colleges. He's had many poems and short essays published in small publications. He's become quite a spiritual person and shares his insights in print.

He's written his life story in a few different versions, as fiction and non-fiction. His daughter-in-law, a journalist who lives near him, has graciously agreed to help organize all this output and hopefully he and I can each publish our memoirs close together. I already know that we have quite contradictory memories about a variety of things!

It's a joy for me to see how my troubled brother has emerged as a contented and respected elder. He reads and rereads a few inspirational books that really speak to him. He often pairs this reading with exercising, mostly on a stationary bike. Very often when he finishes one of these sessions he lets everyone within hearing distance know: "I feel like a million bucks!" I love to hear that shout!

His offspring and friends turn to him for guidance and support. His mother, who spent her life trying to make him better, died admiring his wisdom and insight. He spent hours just holding her hand. I know from experience there is something special about that touch. Whenever I've felt it I am at peace.

My brother and sister-in-law, Tom & Joan Thomas

Tom with his "boys," from left John, Bob and Phil

Mooreland Hill School

Mooreland was a country day school for grades 7 through 9, then known as junior high. (It has been through several changes since my day, all the way down to a K-5, and finally folded entirely in 2019.) It was a tiny but idyllic school in Kensington, next door to New Britain, with about 20 students when my father started there as headmaster, 30 by the time I graduated in 1948 and 100 when my great-nephew graduated decades later.

A big old converted farmhouse, it included classrooms, upstairs study hall, downstairs dining room (where lunch was served) and Daddy's office just inside the front door. There were a few acres of land where several sports were played.

My father was the dominant figure. As headmaster of a school with a handful of teachers, he also taught English and Latin and coached some of the sports.

When I started there I was surprised to find he had another persona. At home he was always gentle. At school he could be stern. The students respected him and shaped up for him but also loved him, because he was fair and fun. He was not above getting down on the ground to rough-house with the kids despite his bad heart. Then it seemed perfectly normal but now he would probably be accused of harassment or perversion.

He occasionally surprised us with a free day. We would assemble in the study hall in the morning and find out that instead of classes that day we were going out—to a picnic or to play in the snow or…. We loved those days.

Daddy was a fabulous headmaster/teacher. So many of his former students have told me he was their favorite teacher and some say he changed their lives. He was more than a teacher. He was a friend and mentor. I know he made me want to learn and I'm certainly grateful that, thanks to him, I love to read and I have an excellent grounding in grammar and spelling, important tools of my trade.

In addition to English and Latin, which we all studied for three years, we also had French, math, science and history classes.

Some time while at Mooreland I switched from being a bit of a ham to having acute stage fright. I don't have a clue what changed or why. Just suddenly I knew I was unable to get up in front of the class or the school and recite or read. I just couldn't do it. And yet I couldn't admit it to my father so instead I lied.

I was supposed to present a paper in front of the school. After considerable agonizing about how to get out of it, at the last minute I hid the paper and said I had lost it.

(I never recovered from stage fright, despite required speech classes later at prep school, but I'm happy to say that now as an adult if I'm asked to speak in public I'm not afraid to say no, I can't do that.)

I was able to say one line in a play. Daddy had been the drama coach at Tabor and he loved to put on plays. I remember appearing as a flower girl in a play-- in French! I remember my one line: "Voulez vous acheter un fleur, monsieur?" That I could handle.

I was never conscious of any difficulty over our dual roles at home and school. I think Daddy treated me the same as all the other kids and I think that was fine with me.

I was not a brilliant student but I was eager to please my father, whom I adored. He wanted me to be a good student so I was. He helped me with homework but I'm sure was scrupulous about doing no more than any other parent would do. And I was never aware of resentment or suspicion from other students when I was on the honor roll all the time. I was never embarrassed by the relationship. He handled what could have been a very tricky situation quite well.

Mooreland had a small newspaper and my father steered me to work on it. Later I learned that he had hoped for a career in journalism for himself. Since that hadn't happened he apparently hoped to interest me.

My mother was a substitute teacher all the years my father was at Mooreland. Unlike my father, whom I remember as always calm and fair, my mother had a temper that was easily fired. She was Irish after all.

I was afraid of her wrath and I was embarrassed when it surfaced in the school room in front of the other kids, especially because she had a way of twisting the situation: We were bad because we made her feel bad!

(I'm sorry to say both Tom and I inherited the Irish temper. His erupted often when he was young. I'm usually too shy to show mine but now and then I scare myself. I've found myself smacking a dog for unruly behavior, then thanking fate that I never had children because I might have done the same to them.)

Some time during their years at Mooreland, according to Mum, Daddy had an affair with a French teacher. Mum discovered it when she found them in Daddy's office. Mum told me this late in her life and I wished she hadn't; I hoped it wasn't true, that she was mentally confused. I idealized my father and resented any information that made him less than perfect.

My last year at Mooreland we were tested by an outside firm to help determine our future course: what kind of college we should attend and what kind of career we should follow. My results determined I should go to a large co-ed university and that I should become a business woman.

I have no idea what those paths were based on but I obviously didn't pay much attention. I proceeded to a girls' prep school followed by a girls' college and then a career in journalism. I should add that those choices were more parental than mine, but I didn't object. I probably didn't even have an opinion.

We had an active sports program at Mooreland and played against other private schools in the area. Though tiny, I was fairly athletic and especially liked baseball and played short-stop.

One season I had a perfect batting average. I hit the ball every time I was at bat until near the end of the season when the coach pointed out that if I kept it up I would have a 1000 batting average for the season. Immediately I started missing. I don't do well under pressure and I am not at all competitive.

After school we often went to "the club," which was on the other side of the playing fields. It was an expensive, exclusively WASP country club with a good golf course. The families of most of the students were members, and we were too. It was one of the perks of being headmaster.

I took a few golf lessons from the club pro but found the game very boring, as I never hit the ball more than a few feet at a time. But I loved to sit at the bar with my friends drinking black cows or brown cows-- coke or root beer with vanilla ice cream. We signed for our drinks and our parents paid for them.

44 Steele Street

In 1948, knowing we would have to leave the farm soon, we had bought a house under construction at 44 Steele Street, New Britain, but it wasn't finished by the time we left the farm so we lived in two loaners while waiting for it to be finished.

I was away at boarding school when the rest of the family moved in. When I came home for Christmas vacation we were there. It is an undistinguished boxy house in an unremarkable section of town. We had lived in much nicer houses in the past and I, already a snob, was a bit ashamed of my new home and neighborhood. It was all we could afford. (I have the figure $11,000 in my head but no idea if that's correct.)

Because of Daddy's health we did not have to make our usual trek to New Jersey that year, to celebrate Christmas with Aunt Emy and Uncle Charles (see The Engelhards on page 10.) That was a relief. But our first Christmas in our own home was hardly a joyous occasion, haunted by Daddy's ailing health. As I remember we had a small tree and tried to be festive without much success.

My father died that summer. One afternoon he walked down the stairs in his pajamas and bathrobe, accompanied by two attendants from the ambulance that waited outside. He was gaunt and gray but he tossed off a jaunty remark with a smile as he walked out the front door: "I'm off to the gallows." I knew then that he knew he was going to die. I never saw him again.

It was 1949. My father was 52. I was 15, a very young 15, a child. Mum didn't want me to see him in an oxygen tent with his head full of tubes. She urged me to go to a house party 500 miles away with girls from my boarding school class. I did, but every time the phone rang there I froze, and eventually I had a message: come home. I didn't know if he was dead or alive.

On the overnight train I stayed in my upper berth the whole trip, afraid of the rowdy soldiers in the car. The family friend who met me at the station drove me to the hospital. When I arrived at Daddy's room I had a very brief glimpse of a spectral body on a bed before Mum headed me off with "I don't want you to see him like this." I waited at Steele Street. Mum waited at the hospital. After a couple of days she came home and said "It's over."

I had nothing to wear to a funeral. Mum and someone else, an aunt or cousin, took me shopping. We bought a navy blue silk dress. It was the first funeral I had ever attended. The casket was closed, thank god, but it was right there at the front of the church and I was in the first pew with my mother and brother. I sobbed throughout the service.

It was a long summer. I tried to be a pal to my mother and she tried to be a pal to me. There was no such thing as a swimming pool nearby but she drove me miles away to public pools a couple of times when the heat was terrible.

An uncle I had not seen for years, my father's oldest brother, came to visit. My heart stopped as I came down the stairs and saw Uncle Lyman in the living room. He looked just like my father. It was like seeing a ghost.

Oddly, Tom is seldom a part of my early Steele Street memories. I guess when I was there he was away at school or working out of town and our paths rarely crossed.

The fall after Daddy died Tom was in a terrible auto accident. He was driving and there were three teenage passengers, all badly injured. But he must have been the worst. He was in a coma for a week, then in traction for months, with many broken bones, including I think all his toes.

The first time I saw him he was in the hospital with all his limbs suspended. I don't remember whether he was still in the coma or awake. I don't remember whether I was called home especially or it was vacation time. I was sure I would never again see him as I knew him. How could anyone recover from that!

The next time I saw him he was at home, downstairs in the dining room in a hospital bed. I still thought he could never recover completely. I think Mum was doing most of the nursing. She was also working as headmistress of Mooreland Hill School! She had agreed to take over Daddy's job for a year while they searched for a new headmaster.

Not surprisingly, Tom was grouchy and Mum was short with him. I think that scenario continued for quite a while. It was quite depressing. I wonder how they got through it.

I think I felt worse for Mum than for him. To lose her husband and then a few months later go through this with her son.

Now I wonder how anyone survives adolescence. I probably got my driver's license the minute I turned 16, but of course I didn't have a car. My friend Trudy did have a car but she had no license. I drove hers.

On summer nights Trudy and I met up with other teenagers at Ferndale's, an ice cream shop on the outskirts of town. We ate ice cream, we talked, we flirted and then we got into our cars and hot-rodded it home. It was just a two-lane road, one in each direction. I raced against one or two cars full of boys down that road. I hope my memory exaggerates but as I recall it we went very fast and we took alarming chances. I was exhilarated by the speed and danger, which surprises me now. Now I'm a real chicken on the road.

Mum was often out of town, accompanying Aunt Emy to a spa or function. One of her absences coincided with a school vacation when Tom and I were both home and so were a lot of our friends. We had a party. We raided the liquor closet and stayed up all night. I don't know if I had ever watched the dawn before. I went out on our little side porch to see the sun rise and was enchanted. I was oddly sober and everyone else seemed so too. The next day we coolly added water to the bottles, assuming Mum would never notice the pilfered booze. Amazingly, nothing was ever said.

When Daddy was alive there wasn't any drinking in the house. Maybe if we had company drinks were served but I have no memory of alcohol then.

Mum made a point of introducing me and Tom to alcohol at home so that we would know what it did to us and not make fools of ourselves outside. I thank her for that.

Mum had trouble sleeping after Daddy died and started drinking to knock herself out. A friend introduced her to a cheap rye, Guckenheimer, which she bought by the case. She kept a bottle under her night table.

I loved decorating my own bedroom for the first time. It was all pink—walls, bedspread, dotted Swiss curtains that I made myself, a bedside table and bookcases that I made out of orange crates and painted pink. I was really pleased with myself when I discovered a cheap way to "frame" pictures. I simply taped them to the wall with brightly colored Mystic Tape.

Meals were never memorable at 44 Steele. Mum was not a cook, or an eater. Like most people in the 50s she believed dinner should include meat or fish, potatoes and a vegetable, and she did her best to serve us such a meal every night. Luckily for her, frozen foods were coming into their prime and pressure cookers had been invented.

We had a frozen vegetable every night when she discovered that all she had to do was open the package, dump it in the pressure cooker, turn the heat on high and wait for the pressure to blow off steam three times. And there were frozen French fries that just had to be heated in the oven. Hamburgers were our most frequent meat and, like the vegetables, overdone. No wonder none of us cared much about food! No wonder we were all skinny!

Our favorite meal was Sunday Night Supper, when we had Cheese Dreams. Until recently I thought Mum had invented them: open sandwiches layered with cheese, tomato, onion and bacon and cooked under the broiler. That's the only food I recall really enjoying at home.

We ate in the kitchen most of the time. Mum's dining room furnishings were far too elegant for family.

Guests were of course served in the dining room, on a large mahogany table with a lace tablecloth, the good crystal and china and silver. We had an overwhelming array of silver; between wedding gifts and boarding school memorabilia, my parents had acquired enough tea sets and serving trays to furnish a palace.

Mum considered dinner parties a social obligation and whenever she had one she was a basket case. The meals centered around some meat roasted in the oven, the timing of which was always a matter of great anxiety.

Every pot and pan, every serving piece came out for company. As the things were no longer needed they were stashed out of sight-- in the garage, on the breezeway connecting the kitchen to the garage, or on the basement steps off the kitchen. Exhausted by the end of the evening, she was unable to cope with the overwhelming clean-up. The morning after we retrieved greasy pans and plates from all over the house.

I inherited her lack of cooking skills and her ineptness at entertaining.

After Mum remarried and moved out of 44 Steele, she gave the house to Tom, who was also about to get married. That was 1959 and now, 53 years later, they are still there.

With the newlyweds there, I had little connection to the house for the next 36 years. When I went "home" it was to my mother's new home. I always stopped in to see Tom and Joan and their family but our visits were short and we didn't really get to know each other until they started visiting me in St. Croix.

Some time during the years when their three kids were growing up they started serving Christmas dinner and other holiday meals at Steele Street and the tradition continues. The house bursts with relatives; we're up to four generations. It's a noisy, chaotic celebration, the opposite extreme to those pathetic holidays the three of us observed in the early years. Mum wouldn't miss it, no matter how bad the weather. Even when she couldn't see or hear and didn't really know what was going on and had to be carried up the front steps in her wheelchair, she wanted to be in the living room in the midst of the melee. Some grandchild or great-grand would devote a couple of minutes to her and she would be thrilled.

Since her death, 44 Steele Street has once again become my home away from home. I usually visit twice a year for a couple of weeks and know that "my room" is always available whenever I want to come. I love that.

Emma Willard School

After graduating from Mooreland, there was no question but that I would go away to boarding school. The local high school was not even considered. Its reputation was way beneath my parents' scholastic requirements.

Some Mooreland graduates went on to private schools within commuting distance but most went on to boarding schools.

I entered the sophomore class of Emma Willard School in Troy, N.Y., in the fall of 1948. It was and still is a prestigious girls' prep school, the first women's higher education institution in the United States, founded by women's rights advocate Emma Willard in 1814. My parents considered it tops academically and it offered me a good scholarship, so there I went.

The EW campus looks like a college or university, with stately stone buildings and green lawns, and has been the setting for two movies that I know of: "The Scent of a Woman" and "The Emperor's Club". The buildings were dark and formal inside, with leaded glass windows. They seemed cold and forbidding to me. So did the women who ran the school.

I was a very young 14, physically, socially and emotionally. And I was very homesick; except for my brief summer camp experience I had never been away from home before. I wasn't used to regimented life and I was worried about my sick father.

Also I soon discovered that I wasn't as smart as I thought I was, having always been on the honor roll. With new subjects, new teachers and new peers, I was shocked to find I had to work hard to keep up.

My housemother, who should have been a comfort, proved otherwise. She scolded me-- in front of other girls-- for not having enough underpants in my laundry bag! Even that was regulated!

We were required to arrive at school with a certain number of uniforms: four gingham check dresses for spring and fall, two wool jumpers with six white blouses for winter, and a few silky dresses for dinner. In addition we were required to bring seven sets of underwear, stockings and socks, one for each day of the week. We put our dirty laundry outside our doors once a week. Damn if the housemother didn't root through it to make sure we were changing every day!

When I went home for the Thanksgiving holiday I begged not to be sent back. I was, but with the promise that if I still felt the same at Christmas time they might let me stay home. Wise parents. How did they know that a month later I would be more or less comfortable with my new school?

Polly, one of my best friends from New Britain, also started at EW that year but, instead of embracing my dear familiar friend, I turned against her almost immediately. She took to the school much better than I did and emerged a natural leader in no time. For some reason I held that against her. I guess it couldn't have been too bad because we must have traveled back and forth together, but we certainly never again had that closeness we had as kids. (Our other best friend, Ann, went to Northfield.)

I made it through my sophomore year and was a changed person when I returned for my junior year. My father had died that summer and without him to please I stopped striving academically and began to look for other forms of satisfaction.

In the authoritarian, prissy environment of my girls' school my behavior was pretty tame stuff: skipping assembly, sneaking off campus with some other girls to skinny dip in a pond, exploring a forbidden tower. But I enjoyed being a rule breaker.

I broke enough rules to be put on probation. Mum was informed. When she phoned me she made me feel guilty—not so much for breaking rules as for being an ungrateful scholarship student. She thought I ought to show my gratitude for being there by being a role model. I realized she had a point and was properly contrite but I think I continued to act out in my very timid way.

I also dyed a blond streak into my dark hair.

We were all required to do a sport each season. In the fall I chose soccer as a little less intimidating than field hockey. Our team colors were purple and green. I was a purple.

Classes are a blur. I liked an English teacher, Miss S, who made literature, especially sonnets, interesting. Along with all the other students I mocked the biology teacher, Miss R, for her discomfort when teaching about the reproductive system and her euphemisms for private parts.

I doubt that I appreciated it at the time but now I am really grateful for the core curriculum taught there, especially that art and music were included. Each year history, literature, art and music were covered in a different era, something like the middle ages sophomore year, the Renaissance junior year and modern ages senior year. I had never been exposed to art or music before. Now they are two major joys of my life and I wonder if I would have discovered them on my own.

I also discovered jazz and the Charleston senior year. There was a 20s revival and we all learned the Charleston. Somehow I discovered and loved Stan Kenton's very dissonant "progressive jazz". Probably because it reflected my rebellious mood.

I started smoking in Maine while visiting a friend there during the summer. I was probably 16. I was too chicken to smoke on campus (that was cause for suspension) but I did sneak some smokes when home on vacations, hiding it from Mum, of course.

Sunday chapel was required and we had some of the country's most famous theologians as guest speakers. I was ripe for religion and was thrilled by some of the sermons but I think I was moved intellectually more than spiritually and the glow never lasted. I never followed up at all when I left EW. Except for weddings and funerals, I rarely set foot in a church for the next 40 years.

I had worked on the school newspaper at Mooreland. I knew my father had hoped I'd become a journalist so I joined the staff of the EW paper too. I don't remember a thing I wrote for it and I'm quite surprised to see in the EW yearbook that I was the editor of "The Clock." I didn't think I had an extracurricular achievement in any field or had ever held an office. My hometown friend Polly, meanwhile, was running the school!

In retrospect I am very fond of many of the girls and a bit surprised that I had many friends. We played a lot of bridge on the floor of the dorm and we had a common room with a phonograph where I played my Stan Kenton records and we danced the Charleston.

Many of my schoolmates were from wealthy families and upscale towns. Most of them were much more sophisticated than I and many were debutantes. Many had boyfriends at home and led fairly normal social lives when they were home. My industrial town did not produce debutantes and I certainly never had a boyfriend.

There was no dating at the school of course but we did have occasional dances with boys' schools at which we were paired by height and chaperoned by teachers who made sure we stayed a foot from our partners—"the 12-inch rule".

I had to take a speech class, which was pure torture for me. My stage fright was full-blown by then and I couldn't speak for a minute without sweating and gulping and my heart pounding. (Seventy years later nothing has changed.)

I had braces on my teeth much of the time I was at EW. In my year book picture I am unsmiling and obviously with a mouthful. In elementary school I had a removable brace, like a retainer, which apparently hadn't worked. Now I had the works, railroad tracks I called them: a steel band around each tooth, all connected with wires that were tightened periodically.

I was taken to nearby Albany to see an orthodontist. During the summer I rode the train from Connecticut to New York City to see a different dentist. He was a teaching dentist and I always had several students peering in my mouth when I went there.

This had to be very expensive. My mother certainly made a lot of sacrifices trying to make me beautiful. I'm sorry to say that instead of thanking her for trying to improve my appearance I chose to be humiliated that she thought I wasn't pretty enough as I was. I frequently behaved contrarily in a bid for reassurance. Now I'm grateful she went ahead anyway and did what she correctly assumed I would appreciate later.

We rarely were allowed off-campus. I have no idea what the town of Troy looks like. A couple of times I walked to an ice cream shop with a chaperoned group and that's about it.

We were taken to some cultural events in Albany. I remember a concert hall and a symphony orchestra. That's where I learned that one doesn't clap after movements, only at the end of a classical piece.

The school was run by a pair of older women, who made no attempt to befriend the students. I was in the headmistresses' home only once that I recall, during my senior year when a Wellesley admissions person came for interviews and tea with the girls who had applied there.

I think she had something to do with scholarships too because I credited my braces for getting me into Wellesley with a good scholarship. The only conversation I remember is her sympathetic disclosure that she also had worn braces her senior year in high school. The good news was that those braces were finally removed just before I started college.

My liberal inclination started to surface at EW when a World Federalists club started and I became a member. Today I'm surprised to find via Google that the "global citizens movement" still exists. I hadn't heard anything about it since I left the school but I'm glad to find I was in good company. Other advocates included Albert Einstein, Mahatma Gandhi and Martin Luther King Jr.

One Sunday noon during my junior year, Mum made a surprise appearance. As we gathered in the living room of the dorm before dinner, there she was. She had been summoned for an interview and was offered the job as head of the lower school. (She turned it down and stayed on teaching at Mooreland for the next 10 years, until she remarried and retired.)

Apparently she didn't know we were allowed to wear our own clothes on Sunday and was embarrassed that I was wearing my dinner uniform while most of the other girls were in smart dresses and suits. I don't remember that it bothered me that I didn't have anything else to wear but Mum immediately sent me a nice blue suit. I remember feeling quite sharp in it.

I guess I was happy enough while I was there, but in retrospect I hated it-- the coldness of the authority figures and the impersonality of the rules. After going back once for my 10th reunion I was really turned off. Polly and I went together, she from Philadelphia and I from Manhattan.

We were the only two career girls in the group and the only ones without children. Polly had a husband but, though she didn't announce this, she was about to divorce him. We both felt out of place and left early, laughing at our dumpy classmates in their frumpy clothes. I was the freak, dressed in my New York suit and heels, my hair coiffed and my face made up.

For many years after that I would have nothing to do with the school. As my 50th reunion approached I softened. I recognized how much I appreciated the education and the core curriculum and what fond memories I had of the girls. I went and had a good time.

Wellesley College

I went to Wellesley College because it offered me the best scholarship and because my mother had gone there (Class of 1926). I had also been accepted at Smith and Middlebury but didn't give them much attention.

I knew that Wellesley was one of The Seven Sisters (top women's liberal arts colleges) but I have to admit I was oblivious to its wider reputation as one of the most outstanding colleges of any gender in the country. (It's still going strong, the third best liberal arts college in the U.S. in the 2019 *U.S. News and World Report* and the most heavily endowed, $2 billion!)

I did appreciate the great environment, a sprawling country setting with a pretty lake just outside the attractive "village" of Wellesley, which is just 13 miles west of Boston and Cambridge. It was a 2 1/2-hour drive from New Britain.

My mother drove me to my dormitory on my first day of college. Noanette was one of the big old houses in the village where most of the freshman lived then. I shared a large room on the second floor with Margie, whom I met for the first time that day. She was tall and outgoing and confident and seemed to know everyone already.

Life Magazine was doing a feature story about our class starting college, focusing on a girl in a dorm across the street. She and her friends were all pretty and all wore Bermuda shorts. The shorts were new that year and a lot of the girls were wearing them, but I had never seen them before.

We walked or rode bikes to the campus for classes. My mother had told me that's what caused a phenomenon known as "the Wellesley stride."

I knew from the beginning I would major in English but few classes in any subject in any year stand out in memory. My English courses were mostly poetry and literature but I had some writing classes too. I took French every year, continuing the subject I had started in 7th grade. In a Bible History class I learned that the Bible is not history and lost my innocent "faith". I liked psychology and sociology.

I'm not sure when I decided to become a journalist but Wellesley, being a liberal arts college, did not offer courses in such a practical field. English was the closest I could get. But, I'm ashamed to say, I was very blasé about the whole academic scene. It's amazing how few memories I have of classes, homework etc. I think I realized early on that I didn't have to work very hard to keep a decent average and that was good enough for me.

I had never had a boyfriend before going to college. In just a few weeks I met Dick, from Harvard. We met at a "mixer," a quaint custom that brought boys and girls together from their one-sex schools. I was so shy I had to be dragged to the dance, but luckily Dick fell in love with me right away and saved me from further social trauma.

A late bloomer, I had had very little experience with boys, a few awkward dates, a few awkward kisses. Before I went off to college my mother had informed me it was alright to kiss but not to allow anything else until I was married. She easily convinced me that sex was bad and sinful and that if I indulged I would be a big disappointment to her. My fear of her wrath kept me a good girl for many years.

And, I will add, in 1951 I think virginity before marriage was still the norm in my milieu. I remember being terribly shocked to learn that a senior was being thrown out because she was pregnant.

Dick and I "went steady" for over a year and I think I always knew he was not "the one" for me but I didn't know how to break it off. He was so sweet and so in love and I loved being loved so I just let it go on.

He was a scholarship student too. We did free things at Harvard like football games and dorm parties. He was in Eliot House and had a black roommate, a rare thing at that time (1951).

Tom Lehrer, the satirical song writer and performer, was at Harvard then and we often heard him entertain. I loved his wonderful clever songs. The only lyrics I remember now are "I've got tears in my ears from lying on my back in my bed while I cry over you."

Dick took the bus out to Wellesley during the week. We "studied" together in private places and necked. He gave me his Exeter class ring which I wore with a wad of tape to make it fit on my finger or on a chain around my neck. I liked the secure feeling of "belonging" to someone and I liked having other people recognize that I was loved.

Even though she didn't like my choice of boyfriend (why did I have to pick a poor poet?), Mum was generous about making sure I had some nice clothes to wear on dates. Lord knows how she found such perfect clothes or how she afforded them, but she sent me a couple of dresses I loved so much I can still see them clearly: a princess style teal wool dress with long sleeves and jewel neckline, and a red velvet strapless gown with white fur trimming the top.

Sophomore year all my class moved onto the campus. Margie and I moved into Shafer Hall on the Quadrangle. We had two small rooms across the hall from each other on a short corridor off the back stairs, probably old maids' rooms. We made one into a bedroom and the other into a living room/study.

I had taught myself to type at home; there was no such practical course at Wellesley of course. I made a little money typing papers for others—at 20 cents a page I think it was.

I don't know when I started working for the college newspaper or what I did on it before I found my niche as a drama critic. With absolutely no knowledge of what I was talking about, I wrote cruel, acidic reviews of college theater productions.

I especially panned the boyfriend of one of my best friends, who was president of the theater group. He traveled from Harvard to play male roles in our college plays. For some reason Barbara never held this against me. I was later a bridesmaid at her wedding to this same actor, and a year after that became godmother to their first child! How could I look them in the eye! How could they forgive me!

(I was subsequently a bridesmaid far too often. The attic at 44 Steele was the depository for what I considered ugly pastel taffeta dresses with matching shoes and hats. Each wedding took place in a church where the bride wore a white gown with train and veil and was attended by multiple bridesmaids and ushers, with an expensive reception following at a country club or similar venue. I never understood the attraction of all the rituals. When the hippies came along in the 60s and got married in meadows wearing flowered dresses and bare feet, I thought that's more like it.)

At one point later in life when I referred to my college years I joked that I majored in Harvard and minored in MIT. That was a gross exaggeration of course. I didn't have that many boyfriends, but they might have been more important to me than my classes.

Once I finally broke up with Dick, I concentrated on other boys and skiing. My junior year especially, when I had a "ski bum" boyfriend in Stowe, VT, I might have spent more time off-campus than on.

I and my friend Dana would scan the bulletin boards for rides to Stowe, our chosen destination because Dana worked there Christmas vacations and acquired enough ski lift passes to get us through the season! We often drove all night, skied and partied all weekend, then drove all night again to get back for Monday classes. One of our rides was and old hearse.

There were times when I came back just long enough to take a test and/or write a paper, then turned around and went to Stowe again. I was so gung-ho I once skied in 25 below zero weather. There were just a few of us on the slopes that day.

My ski bum boyfriend was an "older man," maybe 25, a journalist who was taking a break. He had a job at the cheap dormitory-style lodge where we always stayed. Already thinking that journalism might be my career, I was thrilled to know a real reporter.

We spent evenings drinking Old Forester bourbon. I had never drunk much of anything alcoholic before but I turned out to be a quick learner.

The day he finished his job there he drove me back to college before returning to his real job with United Press International somewhere in the south.

As we pulled away from the lodge there was a big racket. The other ski bums had attached tin cans and a Just Married sign to the car!

When he got back to work he wrote me long letters on his office's teletype machine. Each envelope contained feet of continuous yellow paper printed with purple ink. These entertained my whole dorm corridor.

That was a busy year for me socially. At one point I had three Dicks calling me. One introduced me to fraternity parties at MIT. He was handsome and charming, a Virginian with money, and I tried to get interested. My mother would have been thrilled! Another attempted to seduce me in what today would be called "date rape." I was so adamantly not going to let that happen that he finally gave up.

The best date of my college career was a weekend in New York City. I stayed at the Wellesley Club and my date stayed in a hotel with his parents, who were visiting from the Midwest. We spent an evening at a bar in Greenwich Village listening to one of my favorites: Louis Armstrong.

In all the years I went to boarding school and college my mother never mentioned the hardships she must have endured to help me financially. My scholarships covered most of my expenses but Mum must have paid for my clothes and books and transportation out of her own pocket and I know that teaching at Mooreland she made pennies. The most Daddy had ever made was $3000 a year, and he was headmaster. She must have made even less. How did she do it!

Years later when it dawned on me how cavalier I was about being supported, she was just as bewildered as I was and had no idea how she managed it.

I did odd jobs at college now and then but never earned more than pocket money. Once when I needed more I applied for a job through a college office. For some reason my mother was contacted and she called me-- furious that I had gone to them instead of her! I had hurt her pride!

As graduation neared I had to start looking for a real job. Since I had decided that journalism was my field, despite my lack of education or experience in the field I naively sent applications to all the top newspapers in the country, from the *New York Times* to the *San Francisco Chronicle*. Journalism was quite a glamorous career then and of course none of the big papers would even consider me. I can't believe how stupid I was.

After graduation I went home to continue my fruitless pursuit.

Summer Jobs

The summer I was 16, just before I went to college, I had my first job. I made minimum wage, 75 cents an hour. I was an assistant at the reception desk at the local hospital. I took each new patient in a wheelchair to the admissions office, then to X-ray for chest shots, then into the elevator and up to his/her assigned floor.

It was 1950, and elevators were not automatic then. An operator had to turn a lever to make it go up or down and to guide it to a stop at a level equal to the floor outside. If the elevator operator was on a break I had to deal with the levers myself and get my patient to his floor.

Some of the patients were very sick, and some of them were very pregnant. The women in labor terrified me. I was afraid they would deliver in the elevator when I was the only other person around. I was scared that I wouldn't be able to line up the elevator properly and that the bumpy exit would bounce the baby out. I was so relieved when I was able to turn my patient over to a capable nurse and run off the maternity floor with my empty wheelchair.

But I passed a couple of delivery rooms on my way. The blood that I saw and the screams that I heard horrified me. They probably contributed to my lack of any maternal yearnings.

My boss must have been a sadist. At noon, when the switchboard operator left for her lunch hour, I had to fill in for her. Again, nothing was automated yet. The operator was responsible for connecting the caller to the called by plugging in the correct two cords out of a rat's nest of dozens. There was plenty of opportunity for error. In those days, long before 911, one called the hospital and asked for an ambulance when there was a medical emergency. I lived in terror of misdirecting a call in a matter of life or death.

There's no question that my first job was the most stressful I ever had. Luckily for me, my mother was also unsettled that summer. After doing my father's job for a year while the school searched for a new headmaster, she was taking courses to get certified for a teaching position in public schools. (She never did teach in a public school. She continued to teach at Mooreland until she remarried 10 years later and retired.)

Not a great student, she studied late into the night at her desk in the bay window of the living room at 44 Steele. One night I sleep-walked down the stairs into the living room and was on my way out the front door when Mum said "Where are you going?" "To get the doctor," I replied.

The summer after my freshman year at Wellesley I worked in the accounting office of a factory. The American Hardware Co. was one of many factories that gave our town, New Britain, Connecticut, the nickname of "Hardware City of the World." I got the job because the president of the company was a friend of the family, not because I had any skill that would qualify me for a job.

I operated an adding machine, the precursor to the calculator. There was no such thing as memory in those pre-computer days. I entered a number, pulled a lever, then entered another number, ad infinitum. When I finished a long, long column of numbers I pressed the total key and hoped for the best. I have no idea what the numbers signified that I was adding up but I made many mistakes. If my total was off I had to do the whole thing over again. It was torture.

There was no air conditioning and the factory was boiling hot but women were required to wear stockings. I wore them with the checked gingham dresses that had been my school uniforms at Emma Willard. I guess I didn't have anything more appropriate.

Fairly early in the summer I was invited to Long Island for a weekend by Judy, a college classmate. The highlight of the visit was a swim at Jones Beach, where I got chilled. I guess that's how I caught polio.

When I got home I thought I had the flu but I called the family doctor and when he heard my symptoms included a stiff neck he came right over. The good old days of house calls.

Somehow he contacted Mum, who was in Rhode Island with Aunt Emy. I was quite surprised to see her arrive home in a taxi (from Rhode Island!) And surprised when an ambulance came to take me to the hospital for a spinal tap (they needed Mum's permission for that) and very surprised to be told I had polio! "But I'm not paralyzed!" I protested. "And we hope you never will be", the doctor replied.

Poor Mum, I thought. A son crippled with cerebral palsy and now a daughter maybe crippled with polio. I was afraid she wouldn't be able to handle it. I truly seemed to be more worried about her than me!

Throughout our childhood our parents were paranoid about polio. We weren't allowed to swim in public pools or even go to the movies in the summer for fear of contracting the dread disease. But by the time we were in our late teens we were considered out of danger. Polio (also known as Infantile Paralysis) was considered a childhood disease. My getting it at 18 took us all by surprise.

They hustled me back into the ambulance and off to Hartford Hospital, where there was an isolation ward for polio patients. There I stayed for a week, flat on my back, nauseated, aching all over but never in terrible pain like some of my ward-mates, also adults.

Our bodies were covered with steaming hot blankets at least twice a day. I believe that was the only treatment I got. The "iron lung" kept the worst cases alive.

No visitors were allowed. Luckily, I was on the ground floor and there was a window near my bed and Mum was not afraid to come to it. We could talk. I'm sure she wasn't supposed to be there but for once I was grateful for her imperious disregard of rules. I was usually embarrassed that she considered herself above the rest of the world, but in this case I was so happy to see her I was willing to overlook her arrogance.

I asked her to try to contact my boyfriend Dick. He worked summers as a forest ranger in Colorado and we wrote each other almost daily. I had only a post office box number for him. Somehow she was able to get him on the phone. That was not the first nor last impossible favor I ever asked of my mother and amazingly she usually produced and she never complained. And I never appreciated the effort.

When the endless week was over I still had no paralysis and I was apparently no longer contagious so I was released. I had to stay in bed at home for most of the rest of the summer, very gradually adding small activities.

We had recently acquired our first TV. It was 1952. Mum generously donated it to my sickroom upstairs. Garry Moore was the host of a daily game show that I enjoyed. I was so grateful for the entertainment I was in love with Garry Moore!

I was able to go back to college on time. I did some exercises for a few weeks or months and then could forget I ever had polio. I have scoliosis—a curved spine—that might or might not be a result of polio. Otherwise I got off Scot free.

The Salk vaccine was available three years later.

The good thing about that summer was that I never had to go back to my job at American Hardware.

The summer before my senior year I went to Montana with my classmate Dana, whose aunt knew the owners of a small dude ranch who hired us to work for the summer as maids.

We took a road trip to get there with two other classmates who had jobs in the west, one of whom had her father's car for the summer.

Our itinerary zig-zagged to wherever we could get a free night—staying with friends and relatives more or less along the way. (A major detour was to Minneapolis for a free night with a college classmate.) On the couple of nights we had to resort to motels we rented only one room, taking turns sleeping on the floor. We ate beans out of cans.

The ranch job fizzled out because of a recession, causing all the expected dudes to cancel, but the owners let us stay on for a month or so, hoping someone might appear. Dana and I shared a cabin in the woods, where it was so cold Dana had to start a fire in the wood stove before I would even get out of bed.

She had a little romance with a 16-year-old helper on the ranch and I had one with a cowboy, the owner's son-in-law, when his wife and children took a little vacation. I'm not very proud of that but his interest took me by surprise and I did have a crush on him.

Halfway through the summer we were let go; it was obvious there was not going to be any business that summer. We hitched a ride to Yellowstone Park and got jobs as chambermaids, which lasted just a couple of days when we discovered that the tips we were expecting to get in lieu of salary did not materialize. The only money we saw was whatever change we swept up from the cabin floors.

We moved on to the Grand Tetons but didn't find work there either so decided we had to go home. Dana bought a train ticket to Boston, where she lived with her aunt.

I had only enough money to get to Cleveland. My roommate Margie lived there so I figured I could borrow from her. When I phoned her from the train station there I found she was away on vacation but somehow I knew the name of the bank where her father was a bigshot so I went there. I find it hard to believe now that I was so clever but I managed to borrow from him enough to get home. Now I wonder if I ever repaid him.

Back at college that fall I took a course in short story writing. My first piece was a love story featuring a cowboy. The teacher humiliated me but taught me a great writing lesson when she commented in front of the whole class: "Your cowboy talks like a Wellesley girl".

II
MY CAREER IN JOURNALISM
1955-1972

New Britain Herald

I started my journalism career at the bottom of the ladder. Thanks to my mother who made a call for me, I was hired as a proof reader on my hometown paper, the *New Britain Herald*, which is just about all I was qualified for.

It was not exactly the window-on-the-world job I had dreamed of, but the editor/publisher let me ease my way into the city room very soon. It was pay-back time. He believed my father's personal attention at Mooreland Hill School had straightened out his son, and he was willing to take chances with me. Thus I spent the next two years working there, living again at 44 Steele.

First I was allowed to help the society editor with her weekly page. I wrote about wedding gowns of Alencon lace week after week and who gave parties for whom. In 1955 this was an elitist page. Only the cream of society made it, and that meant only WASPS.

I parlayed one of these social notes into a little article that the city editor thought was terrific. My lead was: "Mrs. RSB of T Road is New Britain's hostess with the mostest, according to ....." about some award she had won. With that I got my first byline on a real paper.

I was promoted to obituary writer and encouraged to find feature stories. Soon I was asked to start a weekly feature column, With Our Teenagers. I interviewed high school students who stood out for various reasons. Polaroid cameras were brand new and the editor gave me one so that I could take my own pictures to go along with my story. I was a photo-journalist! And then I was an editor too, when the paper started a women's section and I was put in charge of those two pages daily. All this in about a year!

Modern Living was mostly canned features and recipes but I added whatever local photos and stories I could find.

I was a gung-ho reporter even outside my beat, chasing fire engines and going in to work on my day off if there was a big story like a flood. I wrote up a civil rights case: a local musician then living in New York had rented an apartment in the city but when the landlord discovered his roommate was black he kicked them out. This was 1956.

One evening Mum had guests for dinner, a couple, old friends who happened to be passing through. He had a fairly important position in the State Department. He and Mum made me promise that anything he said that night was off the record. I agreed. But at work the following day I couldn't resist telling about my evening with a VIP, and the city desk said write it up. I did.

My VIP hadn't revealed anything earth-shattering, but he had expressed opinions on world affairs and I guess I believed it was a journalist's duty to report any "scoop" she might stumble across.

My article was very short, and poorly done. It was my first "news" story; I didn't know one should write an inverted pyramid, in which facts are stated in decreasing order of importance. I had saved the best for last. The copy editor didn't inform me of my error until <u>after</u> the article was in print. I was chagrined that I had done it wrong and simultaneously horrified that I had done it at all.

Mum was shocked that I had violated their trust, and so was I. It was my first encounter with a classic journalistic dilemma: an individual's right to privacy vs. the public's right to know. My only comfort was that the VIP had left town before the paper came out and was unlikely to ever see a minor article in a small Connecticut paper.

Mum was teaching at Mooreland and she walked to school so that I could have her car! Eventually I bought my own, a vintage English Prefect, for, as I recall, $125.

My salary was $50 a week. It never occurred to me to offer to help with household expenses, and I guess it didn't occur to Mum to ask. I took her so for granted! I was still a child.

Tom must have been living elsewhere-- Florida or New Jersey. I don't remember him being around much during those years.

I got drunk for the first and second time while working at the *Herald* and living at home. I think I had only two dates with a man whose drink was 7&7 (Seagrams Seven, a blended whiskey, and 7Up). We went to clubs and danced and drank a lot of 7&7s. I don't remember feeling drunk but when I got into bed after those evenings and closed my eyes the room spun round and round. I hated the dizziness but it never happened again. From then on I was able to drink as much as I liked without feeling much of anything.

My first job in the real world introduced me to people from a different background than the WASP/preppie/Ivy League/Seven Sisters environment I grew up in, and I found I liked them better. I had been a blossoming liberal in theory; now I actually knew the common man and was happy to be his friend.

I soon had a problem-- a guy named Bill. He was a printer at the *Herald* and I thought I was in love with him. Now I see that the relationship would probably have died an easy and early death if my mother had not objected to him so vehemently. I believe her reaction made me defensive and determined to have my way. The old Forbidden Fruit syndrome.

Mum, a snob, objected to Bill because he was working class, he hadn't gone to college, he didn't speak English perfectly. The elitist attitude offended me, therefore I fought for him.

I found excuses to be out of the house at night so that I could have secret meetings with Bill. I took sewing classes and worked backstage for the community theater. When the activity was over I met Bill and stole an hour or so to park with him.

When Mum did let him come to the house she hid out upstairs in bed with her bottle. We studiously made noise-- the TV, ice cubes, giggling-- to make her think we weren't making out. She assumed that Bill was trying to get me drunk so that he could take advantage of me.

This went on for months, with Mum growing increasingly obsessed. I found hysterical notes detailing his faults and the sins she thought we were committing. We weren't! She had succeeded in brainwashing me so thoroughly that I would be a virgin for a few more years! But she was determined to get rid of him. Finally she led me to believe she would kill herself if I married him.

I had already determined that I had to get out of the house, out of town. I knew my chances of landing a job on another paper were still slim, but I was pretty sure a master's degree from the Columbia School of Journalism would open doors. I had applied. Every time I got another promotion I quickly sent the news to New York. I pressed my case, quite uncharacteristically, because I thought it was my only way out. Finally I was accepted. I think they must have figured anyone that persevering would make a good reporter.

I nursed a huge resentment against my mother that continued for years. Now I know she forgot about her threat soon after, or never meant for me to take it seriously, but she was unstable enough that I accepted it literally. Years later, when I finally was able to bring it up, she had no memory of such intimidation. She had no idea what I was talking about.

While I was working at the *Herald* and living at home, I bought a puppy, another Border Collie that I named Tess II. (I couldn't find another Scottish girl's name in the reference books then available.)

Mum tried to talk me out of it, pointing out the responsibilities of pet ownership, but I blithely ignored her concerns and bought the dog. Then I blithely ignored the responsibilities of pet ownership and basically left it to my mother to cope. All I wanted was puppy love. In a family where people didn't touch, much less embrace, I loved having a puppy on whom I could lavish hugs and kisses and who adored me.

But training? exercising? I must have been 21 or 22, but I was still a child. My house training consisted of putting newspapers on the kitchen floor and shutting the dog in the kitchen at night. I was first up in the morning (I had to be at work at 7:30) and the first thing I did every day was scoop up the poop. One night Tess had diarrhea all over the kitchen floor. Incredibly, I left the mess with a note for Mum: "I couldn't face it. Sorry" and left. I heard about that episode for years later.

I don't think I ever walked the dog. If there were leash laws then they weren't enforced and we just let Tess run free. Border Collies are the black and white dogs bred for sheep herding and, although Tess was never trained to work, the instinct was inbred.

There was an elementary school a block or two from our house where Tess discovered the joys of recess. As the kids came outside to play, she rounded them up, nipping at their heels if they didn't respond fast enough. The principal of the school complained to Mum.

Once again my long-suffering mother handled what should have been my problem. She took Tess to work with her. Mum was teaching at Mooreland Hill. There the kids were in junior high and not so round-upable. So instead of nipping she barked, driving everyone crazy.

When I moved out, I simply left Tess with Mum. Soon after, Mum gave her away, and I was incensed that she got rid of <u>my</u> dog.

Columbia Graduate School of Journalism

The Graduate School of Journalism at Columbia University offered a master's degree in one year. That seemed perfect to me so after two years of working "in the field" I was back in school, class of 1958.

The small class of about 75 mostly men—about a dozen women—included some others with a year or more of experience behind them and a few who were then working on papers in the area at night, but most of them were fresh out of college.

It was a delightful change from my liberal arts college years. Instead of reading books and writing papers and taking exams we pretended we were working journalists-- going out on assignments, reporting and editing the news and publishing a "newspaper" every day. Since Columbia is located in New York City, there was never a shortage of things to report about.

I felt really important attending a meeting of the General Assembly at the United Nations. I have no idea what the subject of the meeting was but I still retain my awe of the instantaneous translators. To think that anyone could do that with such complicated subject matter was beyond my imagination.

My most memorable assignment was to join the press corps accompanying former President Harry Truman when he went for a walk on the sidewalks of Manhattan. I couldn't get near him, of course, so I didn't get a scoop but I got to taste the excitement of chasing the hot news story of the day.

Like most of the "girls" in my class I lived in the graduate women's dorm, Johnson Hall, across the campus from the J School on 116th St.

I became good friends with my next door neighbor there, Marge, who was going to law school. We broke the dormitory law together every cocktail hour by having a couple of drinks from our forbidden flasks of booze. I was still drinking the rye my mother drank, Guckenheimer.

I was at the school most of the day but there wasn't a lot of homework. I got addicted to crossword puzzles. I resented my mother obsessively. I didn't date much at all until late in the year when I had a short romance with a classmate.

Instead of a thesis we had to write a work of journalism, either a "magazine article" or "a newspaper series", based on a course such as foreign policy. The course I chose was called something like *Crisis in the Cities* and my "magazine" piece was about the fictional presidential campaign of Peter Progress, who advocated replacing the 48 contiguous states with about eight regions, each of which had common water sources, etc. I placed the capital of the country in Kansas City, Kansas, because when I folded a map of the country lengthwise, then crosswise, KCK was smack in the middle fold. My candidate's campaign song, to the tune of "Hernando's Hideaway", started:

Oh, Peter Progress is our man,
If he can't do it no one can.

I think I more or less tossed it off. I felt the whole year was sort of a cheat, that our degree wasn't comparable to other masters programs, in which students really had to work hard. But that was fine with me. I wasn't there to learn so much as to get my foot in the door for a decent job.

There was a recession going on when we graduated, and jobs were not that forthcoming. I spent a month or more living with a friend and her new husband in their NY apartment, sleeping on the sofa and typing his graduate thesis while looking for a job. She went to work every day and he worked on his thesis while listening to operas. In return for room and board I typed the long, long thesis he was working on while worrying I would lose my mind being forced to listen to operas all day.

Newsday

Before the summer was over I had a job. It wasn't in New York City but it wasn't far away. I was hired as the copy editor for the women's section of *Newsday*, a serious tabloid with a good reputation on Long Island. Its headquarters were in Garden City. (It's now in Melville. There is now also a branch in New York City.)

At age 24 I was really on my own for the first time. I rented a room in a private home while I looked for an apartment. I had kitchen privileges but I was too shy to use them or mingle with the family. I stayed in my room all the time.

I soon found an "apartment" I could afford, the basement of a small home in Bellerose, almost in Queens, that had been turned into living quarters with a small kitchen and bath. A large green furnace was the centerpiece of my living/bedroom. I loved it. I channeled Rosalind Russell, who played a would-be journalist who lived in a basement apartment in Greenwich Village in the movie "My Sister Eileen."

I was making $75 a week AND I was seeing a psychiatrist in Manhattan once a week. That took a sizable chunk of my salary. I ate canned stew and drank cheap rye. I made my own clothes; I wasn't very good at putting tops and bottoms together and in those days all dresses had a waistline. I hid my wobbly seams with a wide belt.

As copy editor I was in the office every day. Although I was sorry not to be out on the island as a reporter I found I enjoyed the challenges of laying out pages and of writing headlines and captions. They had to fit a certain space and tell the story very succinctly. I was very proud that my "heads" and "cutlines" were often singled out for congratulations on a bulletin board in the *Newsday* city room.

I also stood out as a non-Jew. The women's section was known in-house as "Society" and I was known as "the skinny *shiksa* in Society". (That's Yiddish for gentile and according to Wikipedia is usually derogatory, although at the time I felt it was affectionate.)

I worked there only about a year. My first year on my own turned out to be quite an important one, personally.

I had a weekly appointment with a psychiatrist in the city. I was a basically unhappy person and I guess I hoped a shrink could cure me of that. I was never able to talk to friends or family about what I considered my problems, but I was willing to pay a lot for a professional to listen to me. I cried all through every session but I could not accept his attempts to go deeper, so I quit.

I was drinking enough to start worrying about it. My social life still took place in the city but I had never been concerned about drinking and driving. I'm now appalled to remember the nights I drove home from parties— a trip involving a bridge and several major highways -- knowing I had had too much to drink but trusting that I would be able to do it, and I did. I was then 24 and I continued trusting for 34 more years. I was lucky enough to have only one accident in that period, hurting no one but myself and my car.

That year my mother married Rod Chamberlain, my brother married Joan Gavitt, and I fell in love with a *Newsday* reporter named Dave. He had a very active social life and for a while I was quite aware I was not Dave's first choice of a date. I was called at the last minute when others fell through. I'm surprised I put up with that but eventually I was number one and he fell in love too. I finally gave up my virginity at the ripe old age of 25!

His parents weren't happy about his new girlfriend because I wasn't Jewish and they actually kicked him out of their house, where he was still living at age 30-something.

Our affair was fairly short-lived because everything suddenly changed!

I got rich! Well, I got three thousand dollars, which to me was a fortune at that time. When my mother married Rod she moved into his house in nearby Kensington and gave 44 Steele to Tom so that he and Joan would have a home to move into and would therefore get married. Never showing favoritism, she gave me $3000, apparently the equivalent of what she had given Tom.

I had never had so much money in my life and immediately I knew I was going to Europe. Growing up I felt I hadn't lived until I got to New York. Now that I was there I was sure I wouldn't have lived until I got to Paris.

My mother felt she could and should forbid me from traveling alone. Since I naively dreamed of living abroad for two years or so on my $3000, this was an impasse.

Ultimately my new stepfather had a solution. He had a niece living in Paris and working for NATO. She was willing to have me live with her. So I booked passage on a small Dutch liner, bade a very tearful goodbye to Dave, who planned to move into my apartment and join me in Europe for his vacations, and sailed away.

I recovered quickly enough from my sobbing farewell and enjoyed the attention of two charming men on the Atlantic voyage. I drank schnapps with a Dutch professor before lunch every day and planned to visit him in Holland, and then spent every evening in the bar with a suave American whose European wife was too sea-sick to join him.

The Chamberlains

After my father died, my mother remained single for 10 years. I don't think she was at all interested in dating. The only men I ever saw at the house were gay. One was a brilliant musician who wrote Broadway-caliber musicals for the prep school at which he taught. The other was a flamboyant interior decorator with a delightful sense of humor. They were both very good friends for her.

Rodman W. Chamberlain became my step-father at Christmas time, 1958, after a fairly short courtship. He had been widowed a few years before and he had just retired from his position as vice president in charge of sales for the Stanley Works, one of the top factories in New Britain, "The Hardware City of the World." He loved to play golf and bridge.

I met him early in the courtship, when I made a surprise visit to my mother's house one Saturday. I had started my new job at Newsday on Long Island and I had found an apartment I wanted to rent. But I didn't have enough money to seal the deal because the landlord wanted a month's rent up front and I still had to pay for the current week at the boarding house where I was staying. Naturally I turned to my mother to help me out.

After driving up the Merritt Parkway for a couple of hours I opened the door at 44 Steele Street and there lying on the living room couch was a strange man. My flustered mother made introductions and explained that this friend, Rod Chamberlain, was campaigning for the state senate and he had stopped by to take a nap in between knocking on doors.

I was flustered too and blurted out why I was there-- to borrow money to pay the rent. The man I had never seen before reached in his pocket and pulled out a wad of bills and peeled off the required amount, asking if I was sure that would be enough. My future step-father had endeared himself to me right away. (He did not win the election. He was a Republican, but I forgave him.)

The wedding was held at Craigmore. Unlike my father, who was a quiet man, Rod was gregarious and actually enjoyed participating in the Engelhard milieu, making later visits much more comfortable for my long-suffering mother, who had never had any support from the rest of us.

They had eight good years together before his sudden death following a golf game. He was not shy about announcing his love for her and I think she was happy.

Rod came from a distinguished old Connecticut family; I think there was a governor and a general in his background and there's a Chamberlain School, a Chamberlain Street and a Chamberlain Highway in town.

He had three children several years older than Tom and me-- Rod Jr., Betsy and Steve-- and 11 grandchildren. Much to my surprise—and delight-- my mother was very good as a step-mother and grandmother. She hosted Christmas and other holidays at their small house in Kensington. Any offspring within driving distance came. She became the core of that family, a confidant and counsellor to members of both generations. I was proud of her.

Betsy and I were both delighted to acquire a sister, and the older we got the closer we got, with her traveling from San Francisco to St. Croix to visit me every winter, first with a boyfriend, then with her cousin Phronsie, then with her daughter Lee.

As I write my step-niece Connie and I have just returned from visiting Phronsie at her home on Martha's Vineyard, where she recently celebrated her 100th birthday.

My mother and her second husband, Rodman Chamberlain

My step-cousin Phronsie, left, with step-sister Betsy

European Interlude

Evelyn, my step-father's niece, was a widow about 15 years older than I. I had never met her before. When I arrived in Paris she was living in a small and cheap residential hotel and got me a room there too. I was in heaven.

My tiny room had a window box full of cheerful flowers and a view of some roofs I found charming. It had a bidet and a sink, but the toilet was communal and in the hallway, and the bathtub was in a locked room. One summoned a maid to unlock it and run the water, and once a week was considered often enough.

A maid brought me breakfast in bed every day. I luxuriated in *café au lait*, croissants and almost every morning a love letter from Dave.

It was autumn and I spent the days wandering around the city. At night I met Evelyn for dinner. She knew a number of great little restaurants where we could get a very nice meal and a bottle of wine for about a dollar each. French cuisine is still my very favorite.

Language was a disaster. I had studied French from the 7th grade through college and assumed I would be conversing more or less fluently. Ha! The French are notoriously snooty about other people trying to speak their language and their rudeness at my attempts made me clam right up. To this day I am shy about trying to speak any language other than English and find I have a lousy ear for languages anyway so have given up trying.

Soon I realized I didn't want to be a tourist forever so I started reading the help wanted ads in the English language newspaper, the Paris *Herald-Tribune*. I soon saw a nebulous ad for an English-speaking person interested in education and willing to travel. I didn't want to teach but otherwise I fit the description. I sent off my resume to Heidelberg.

Then I decided to go check out London. I happened to land on the weekend of the annual auto show and there was not a room available in the entire city. I called a Columbia classmate who was in law school in London and living in a convent. She got me a room in her convent for a night or two until the show was over. My cell-like room was very cold and I spent all my time there feeding shillings into a tiny electric heater.

When I got back to Paris there was a message concerning the ad I had answered: call Chuck in Heidelberg! I did and was offered a job vaguely described as having to do with books. He would meet me at the train station there in two days! I went!

I became a saleswoman for an American children's encyclopedia. I worked with a small international crew of young adventurers like me who spent our evenings on American Army bases, going door to door in apartment buildings where servicemen with families lived.

Chuck trained us to get our feet in the door by implying that we were connected to the base school. I preferred to state quite honestly what I was selling and was welcomed into a surprising number of apartments. And I sold a surprising number of 12-volume encyclopedias. They seemed to me quite good and I had no trouble praising them.

I enjoyed the camaraderie of the group. We stayed in *gasthauses* and started working about 5 in the evening, after the men got home from work. We'd sell a few hours, then go back to the *gasthaus* for a late supper and lots of wine.

Our group included another American girl, a Swedish girl and two young Englishmen named Dick, one a poor Cockney and the other upper crust. He spoke a few languages and had worked as a tour guide in Europe.

Upper crust Dick had gone to a university in Lausanne, Switzerland, and invited me to go there with him for a visit with the family he had lived with. So I was treated to a beautiful drive through the Alps and a few days of excellent Swiss food.

We worked in a few different locations. *Gelnhausen* is the only town I remember. Shy little me did so well I was able to buy my boss's car, and when I did that I decided I'd like to go off on my own.

I drove to Munich and happened to arrive during *Oktoberfest*, when Munich celebrates its new crop of beer. The streets were scary with drunks. I stayed in a small hotel and didn't speak to a soul for a week. I drove out to an Army base a few times but didn't sell anything. I rejoined my encyclopedia group, then decided to go back to France and try my luck at the Army bases near Paris. The Cockney went with me.

Evelyn had moved into a nice condominium and invited me to stay with her there. Dick got a cheap room nearby. Evelyn wouldn't let me pay rent but she was Scrooge-like about expenses. Periodically we sat down to figure out how many baths I had had, how much I had ironed, etc., and then she computed my share of the bills.

Dick and I went out to an Army base near Versailles a few times but didn't make any sales.

I got a Dear Jane letter from Dave.

I decided to go home. I had been in Europe about six months.

New York World-Telegram & Sun

When I got back from Europe I quickly found a job. I knew only that I wanted to work for a newspaper in New York City, still a very ambitious wish for a young woman despite the Columbia degree and three years of experience.

There were seven daily newspapers in New York at that time: four standard size (*Times, Herald-Tribune, World-Telegram & Sun and Journal-American*) and three tabloids (*Daily News, Post and Mirror*); The *Times, Tribune and Daily News* hit the streets in early morning, the rest in late afternoon.

Tabloid literally refers to the size of the publication—which in my day was half that of the standard broadsheet. But because most of the smaller papers at that time were all more strident and sensational, the term tabloid was widely used synonymously with "scandal-sheet", "yellow journalism" etc.

I probably would have taken a job on any of them but I got lucky. I answered an ad for the *World-Telegram*. My interview was brief. The women's page editor told me they were looking for a food editor. That was definitely not my field. I told her I knew nothing about cooking. She asked "Do you know the difference between salt and sugar?" I was able to say yes to that and she said "You're hired." Honestly! That's the truth!

I was ecstatic to have a job on "The *Telly*" and soon found out that the food pages were mostly a collection of press releases from manufacturers and distributors and I just had to put them all together in an interesting way.

My byline was Betty Baker. I was the latest incarnation of a fictional food editor who had served the *Telly* for several lifetimes. Occasionally I covered fancy functions introducing new products and came back bearing very nice gifts. Occasionally I was given a non-food assignment, a break I appreciated, especially because I was then given my own byline.

Me aboard the ocean liner Leonardo daVinci, as Betty Baker covering
a food event for the *New York World-Telegram & Sun.*

Eventually I added a weekly column, Recipes of Renown, for which I visited a famous chef in a famous restaurant during its lull in the afternoon. He (they were all men) would prepare one of his specialties for me and my photographer step by step. I kept inserting tablespoons and measuring cups into the process to get a coherent recipe. I also interviewed the owner and the chef for interesting stories to go with the detailed recipe. I was almost always invited to come back for dinner another time with a guest.

The column was a success in the food world and eventually the articles were compiled into a coffee-table book, which I never saw because I had quit by the time it came out. Anyway Betty Baker is the one who got the credit for it. (I don't find it online now. I think it was privately printed.)

I sublet an apartment in Greenwich Village the first few months I worked for the *Telly.* It was one room with a bathroom but no kitchen. I had a hotplate but don't remember eating anything but cucumber sandwiches. I washed dishes in the bathroom sink.

There was a package store around the corner, where I bought a bottle of Canadian Club every week. I had copied my mother's drinking history. Since marrying Rod she had upgraded to CC, and so had I.

I loved being in the Village. My small building was at the end of tiny Commerce Street, really an alley. I was one flight up in the front, facing the alley, the Cherry Lane Theater and a gay bar.

When I had to move out of the sublet, I got together with Pat, another new reporter on the women's page, who had been commuting from New Jersey and we looked for something we could share.

I was attracted to anything unusual. I especially loved mews, the tiny alleys where servants used to live in tiny houses. I even liked the idea of living on a boat. There were a few small marinas on the west side where people did that. I hadn't lived in the city very long but I loved the idea of beating the system—living in the city in a way that wasn't quite of the city. But we couldn't afford anything like that.

Pat and I found a great apartment on the Upper West Side, at 17 West 70th Street, just a few buildings in from Central Park.

We were up one flight of stairs in an old brownstone which had been divided into two apartments per floor. We had the best apartment in the house, the old parlor which had been further divided into a living room, small kitchen, bathroom and tiny bedroom. The latter had originally been the entrance foyer, when there was a flight of stairs from the sidewalk to the second floor. We managed to squeeze in two twin beds and a bureau.

The only closet was in the living room, which was quite attractive. There was a non-working fireplace with a mantelpiece adorned with cherubs and grapes. Two tall windows overlooked a tree-lined street of attractive old brownstones. We paid $125 a month for this charming home that we shared for a couple of years, until Pat married a *Telly* city room reporter and moved out. By then I was earning a decent salary and could afford it by myself.

Our neighborhood was two-faced. Just to the east was lovely Central Park and posh Central Park West, an avenue full of gorgeous, expensive apartment buildings.

At the other end of the block was Columbus Avenue, a rather seedy area. There we patronized the supermarket, the Chinese laundry/dry cleaner, drug store and package store.

"Needle Park," a drug hangout, was nearby. When I came home late at night and asked to be dropped at the corner of my one-way street, taxi drivers often turned the meter off but insisted on driving me around the block so they could drop me at my door.

My mother constantly begged me to move to a better neighborhood and a building with a doorman, but I never felt really threatened. I was perfectly happy.

Pat and I double-dated occasionally. As press, we were often guests of the establishment. Once we were invited to a club where Peggy Lee was singing. The management kept sending over more brandy. We enjoyed the concert well into the early hours. When my date passed out on the men's room floor we put him in one taxi and took another one home.

We were robbed once. Two big Irish plainclothes cops had nabbed two small young Puerto Rican drug addicts as they left our building carrying a few shopping bags. We naturally considered the cops our heroes but I soon changed my mind.

After Pat had moved out and I was there alone, one of the cops came to visit in the middle of the night, drunk. He asked for coffee, which I gave him, then started groping me. He was very big and very strong and had a gun on his hip but I was so determined not to let him rape me he finally gave up and left. I was quite shaken: Who can you call when you're being attacked by a cop? That was the second time I succeeded in thwarting a potential rape.

I lived in that great apartment about five years, during which I made one more trip to Europe, had four more jobs and a few forgettable boyfriends. I did cultural things on my own, buying standing room tickets to plays and ballets, which I loved, trying the opera, which I did not love, and checking out the many museums.

I outgrew my love for making presents; in fact I developed an aversion to the whole idea of gifts after witnessing the frenzy Christmas created—everyone desperate to find something—anything-- to give to a long list of family and friends. That turned me off so much I just stopped giving presents and tried to let everyone know I didn't want to receive them either.

The movie of "Breakfast at Tiffany's" came out. I saw a bit of myself in Holly Golightly. I was smoking then, and now and then at parties I pulled out an expandable cigarette holder, just like Holly's, for laughs.

The *Telly* had a doctor on staff. I went to him for frequent bronchitis and menstrual cramps. All the pills he dispensed came in two colors—like pink for daytime and blue for night. I now realize they were uppers and downers.

I went to Connecticut many weekends. I still considered it "home." My resentment against my mother was wearing off. I caught a train at Grand Central Station after work Friday and returned Sunday night. I enjoyed my new stepfather. The two of us stayed up well into the night playing backgammon and drinking. We played for small money and I tried to win my train fare and often succeeded.

By then most of my contemporaries were married. I had always assumed that I would eventually be too but the more I saw of my newly-married friends the more I realized I might not go there. Especially once they had a baby.

Although they seemed to want to project the image of fulfilled happiness I thought I detected a huge disappointment that marriage wasn't as blissful as it was pictured, an almost desperate terror that they were trapped.

Plus I knew I didn't want to have children; I never felt comfortable around little people, especially babies, and unlike most girls I knew I never baby-sat.

I quit my *Telly* job after about two years to go to Europe again. Pat, her sister Carol and friend Betty were planning a vacation trip to Spain and Portugal and asked if I'd like to join them. Of course I would. But I wasn't interested in just a two-week tour; I would stay longer and travel farther and to do that I had to quit my job.

We had a delightful trip, staying in Portuguese *posadas* and Spanish *paradores*, the old palaces and monasteries that had been re-purposed as moderately priced hotels serving simple but delicious local food. We must have seen every castle, palace and cathedral in both countries. We got used to siestas after lunch and very late dining—about 10 pm.

Pat and Betty flew back to their jobs after two weeks but Carol decided to travel some more with me. I remember nothing of southern France except rather unfriendly receptions. We loved everything about Venice, especially two handsome young men who really did live in a palace on a canal and entertained us there.

The Ladies' Home Journal

On this return from Europe I did not luck into another job so easily and ended up doing something I had sworn never to do—public relations. At least it was for an organization I could respect: the Better Business Bureau. I learned something about non-print journalism because most of my press releases were for radio and television stations.

My PR career was short-lived, thankfully, as I was soon offered a job on The *Ladies Home Journal*, then the top women's magazine in the country. If I couldn't work on a newspaper, this was maybe the next best thing.

The Journal was owned by the prestigious Curtis Publishing Company (which also published *The Saturday Evening Post* and *Holiday*) and had recently moved from its original home in Philadelphia to 666 Fifth Avenue in New York.

I was an assistant editor among some top names in the business and I was suitably impressed.

Assistant Editors didn't write articles, it turned out. We wrote captions and blurbs for articles written by Senior Editors and free-lancers. After a few months I gradually became an unofficial assistant to the Editor-in-Chief, a man, maybe because I was usually available and willing to work late. He didn't really kick in till late in the day.

I was making $10,000 a year, much more money than I ever had on a newspaper-- and enjoying it. Instead of the subway I took taxicabs to work. I bought good clothes at Saks Fifth Avenue and expensive shoes at I Miller. I was introduced to the leisurely three-martini lunch, though in my case I drank CC instead of martinis.

And for the only time in my life I was enjoying weekly hair and nail appointments. It was there at the beauty salon that I heard the news of JFK's assassination. He was my idol.

I had a big crush on one of the Senior Editors. He was a debonair man-about-town, a published author of wit and satire, and a married man who flirted with me and kept inviting me out to lunch. I kept saying yes. He was old enough to be my father. He was commuting from the suburbs, where he still shared a house with a wife he was in the process of divorcing for the second time. But I was smitten and I accepted.

One night after we saw a movie premier together, he had missed the last train home and spent the night on the sofa-bed in my living room. I slept in my bed.

I don't remember any drama involved in the sleeping arrangements but the next day I felt strange and called in sick. For a few days I felt very weak; my legs were like jelly. I thought I might have mononucleosis.

I went to Connecticut to see our family doctor, who found nothing wrong with me but wisely suggested I should see a psychiatrist. I did, and after one session during which I told of my near-affair, I was cured. The shrink had helped me realize that my body was telling me not to take the next step. I was literally dragging my feet. When I returned to work the object of my affection seemed to understand what had happened. We kept our distance, and soon after that the magazine was sold. We were all out of jobs and went our separate ways.

Woman's Day Magazine

I soon got a job on another women's magazine—*Woman's Day*. This was—and still is—a no-frills monthly for down-to-earth family women. I knew nothing about their needs and desires but I wasn't expected to contribute much.

Once again I was an assistant editor mainly writing captions and blurbs for other writers' articles. When I worked there it was owned by Fawcett Publications.

The most interesting thing that happened during my time there was the big blackout of 1965. Most of us had finished our workday around 5 PM and were getting ready to go home when everything went black. When it was clear that this was not a momentary blip, that the whole Northeast was out of light, most of us headed for the stairs, about 14 flights of them.

Our office was in midtown Manhattan. I lived on West 70th St. Of course the subways weren't working. How were we to get home? It was November, and cold.

I lucked out. The boyfriend of one of my co-workers came to pick her up and offered me a ride too. Driving was fun. Traffic lights weren't working, of course, but at every intersection there was a volunteer citizen acting out his version of traffic cop.

As soon as I got home I was sorry I had done so. I couldn't make dinner, I couldn't watch TV or read. I should have gone to a bar and enjoyed the comaraderie that only a crisis generates in the city.

I remembered a blizzard when all the streets were closed to traffic. I ventured out in my ski clothes and met neighbors who had never even nodded before. A few of us lay down in the middle of the street and made snow angels! That was a highlight of my six years in New York.

I was not at all interested in my current work and luckily it didn't last long. I was soon offered my dream job.

New York Herald Tribune

The *Herald Tribune* was my favorite newspaper—almost as prestigious as the *New York Times* but livelier.

My job was in the women's section as usual, but the women's editor, Eugenia Sheppard, was turning it into a feature section with much broader scope. I was encouraged to find my own stories, which I did. None of them had anything to do with food, fashion or furniture, still the mainstays of many women's sections.

As it turned out I was there only a few months because a major newspaper strike closed down all the New York papers in April, 1966. But in the time I was there I finally had the opportunity to find great feature stories, write them, and in some cases see them spread across a full page of the Sunday paper—and the *Trib* was a full-size paper. I saved three of them from March and April 1966.

One was about the architect Philip Johnson and the private underground gallery he had just finished building near his glass house in New Canaan, CT. It was uniquely designed to store his extensive collection of what was then called "Modern Art", mostly giant-sized canvasses by such artists as Lichtenstein, Warhol, Oldenburg and Jasper Johns.

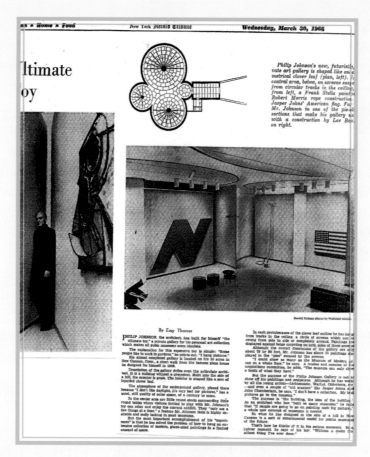

The "scoop" I wrote for the *New York Herald Tribune*.

This article was "a scoop" that delighted my boss. Eugenia Sheppard breezed into our office that Monday morning shouting praise for the piece. She had learned that *Vogue Magazine* was featuring the story in their next issue and was delighted that we had beat them. I owe my mother for this coup; she had met Johnson through a mutual friend and had learned about the gallery through her.

I felt I had to point out to Eugenia that there was an embarrassing typo in the lead sentence—"public museum" came out "pubic museum" but she brushed that off. Nothing was more important than beating the competition!

Another story was about Ivan Karp, "the Father of Pop Art." The article wasn't about the gallery he managed but about his Sunday activity: "rubbling".

He and his wife and a few friends, called "the Anonymous Arts Recovery Society," quietly visited the turn of the 19th century buildings then being torn down to save the beautiful sculptures that had adorned them: "columns, capitals and cornices, gods and giants, nymphs and satyrs."

The Karps' personal favorites were the gargoyles—*genre* portraiture—that the European immigrant stone carvers had slipped in among the neo-classical heads they were hired to create. "They carved each other—warts, missing teeth and all."

The best of their finds were donated to the Brooklyn Museum sculpture garden.

And my final piece, just before the strike, was about Olana, the "castle" built by artist Frederic Church on the Hudson River.

Jackie Kennedy was heading a fund-raising effort to save the house as a museum. It succeeded: it is now owned by the New York State Office of Parks, Recreation and Historic Preservation, assisted by the non-profit Olana Partnership.

The house's creator, Frederic Edwin Church, was a landscape painter of the Hudson River School of the 19th Century, a world traveler who filled his Persian/Italian castle with furniture and artwork from around the world. Olana is Arabic for castle on the hill.

That turned out to be my final piece in New York. When the strike finally ended four months later, only three newspapers survived. The *Herald Tribune* was not one of them.

It didn't take long to realize that my chances of finding another good job in New York—or anywhere on the mainland-- were nil. As one of hundreds of journalists out of work I was among the youngest and least qualified.

I had been to Puerto Rico twice for brief vacations, once during the strike, and loved it. I knew there was an English-language newspaper in San Juan and thought aha! Why not go there! They'd be thrilled to get a New York journalist! I didn't even inquire. I just closed up my apartment and went.

El Mundo

What a blow! I arrived bag and baggage in San Juan and was astonished to find that the English-language paper, the *San Juan Star*, wasn't hiring—not even me!

But I had made my decision to leave the mainland and didn't want to back down so, even though I spoke absolutely no Spanish, I had the *chutzpah* to approach *El Mundo*, the island's leading newspaper, and much to everyone's amazement, I got a job!

San Juan was a swinging tourist destination then, in 1966, and big hotels were competing for big-name entertainment to complement their active casinos, which were quite classy in those days. *El Mundo* thought it was time to cover the entertainment scene.

Most of the entertainers were from the States. Since I was also from the States—and New York at that-- the editors apparently assumed I was qualified to cover them. I had been in only a couple of nightclubs in my life and knew nothing about singing, comedy or girlie shows, but they didn't ask so I didn't tell.

For a year I went to every new show opening. The press were wined and dined at a front row table. I wrote a review of the show and when possible interviewed the star.

Most of the performers were more or less familiar to me, but the only ones that stand out in retrospect are Sammy Davis Jr., Liza Minelli, Johnny Mathis, Jimmy Durante and Robert Goulet. I wrote a review of each show and, when I could get an appointment, also wrote up an interview of the star.

Robert Goulet was my favorite. I loved his performance and wrote a complimentary review. We followed up with a delightful flirty interview and I wrote a delightful flirty feature. Months later I was in New York with my mother. I don't know why but she had rented a suite at the Plaza Hotel and I was planning a party there for my New York area friends that I hadn't seen since moving to PR.

As I walked through the hotel lobby that morning I thought I spied Robert Goulet getting into an elevator. I asked at the desk if he was staying there. They don't reveal such information. I wrote a note inviting him to my party and left it at the desk and sure enough, he arrived when the party was in full swing. He was absolutely charming and we walked around the room arm in arm as he greeted each of my guests.

Anything else entertaining that happened on the island, like filming of a movie with Bob Hope and Gina Lollabrigida, was also my beat. I was with the press corps at the airport when they arrived. A male photographer passed on a beauty secret when he pointed out to me that Gina always raised her chin to the cameras to make herself look younger. I later joined them on location out of town and got a few good quips from Bob.

My work day started at 3 PM, when I wrote up whatever I had covered the night before. My articles were translated into Spanish, of course, and even I could tell they were very basic translations. There was little attempt to capture my carefully crafted prose.

I had enjoyed that job for about a year when the *San Juan Star* finally offered me a job as a reporter on the women's page. I jumped at the chance to write for the English language paper.

San Juan Star

The women's department at the *Star* was small—just three of us—so we shared most of the work. I found I loved doing layouts and was allowed to play around with them and the type, especially on my own stories.

I could write up almost anything I wanted. My features covered everything from a male unisex hair stylist (a brand new thing then) to a new children's zoo. I interviewed women in interesting businesses, men in interesting businesses, art collectors, artists, designers, non-profit presidents, government workers, the governor's wife. I journeyed to a few other islands to write up honeymoon retreats. I did an ongoing series on the unique houses around the island that merited 2-page spreads (with photos of course). Many of these were the architects' own homes and a surprising number of them jutted out from hillsides, cantilevered over woodsy views. Others ranged from historic buildings in Old San Juan to penthouses with precious art collections.

I had the most fun with the pompous food and wine societies. They didn't seem to mind my poking fun at them; they kept inviting me back to their "dress rehearsals". And through them I got to spend a day in the country with the celebrated Craig Claiborne, then food editor of the *New York Times*. (I did not mention to him my time in New York as Betty Baker. Not surprisingly, our paths had never crossed.)

An article I wrote for the *San Juan Star* about the food editor's visit to Puerto Rico.

I was on the *Star* staff for five years and feel that's where I "honed my craft". I give much of the credit to Connie Underhill, the editor of the Sunday Magazine—and my good friend. She rescued me from spending fulltime in the women's department by arranging for me to devote two days a week to the Magazine. The first day I would get my story and the next I would write it up.

It was stressful, as I wrote a long piece for the magazine nearly every week in addition to everything I did for the women's pages, but I loved the magazine job and felt I really blossomed as a writer under Connie's guidance.

She liked/loved almost everything I wrote and I felt she was spot-on on the rare occasions when she felt a phrase or sentence needed work. It was wonderful symbiosis and it continued to work years later when she edited my two books.

Some of the stories I did for her were assigned, others I had to find. They ranged from air traffic controllers to museum curators and a rebel priest. I also interviewed some visiting celebrities: Margaret Whiting, an entertainer since the 1940s, who was doing a show at a local hotel; Dimitri Nabokov, son of author Vladimir Nabokov, an opera singer on island to perform in two operas; Gary Player, the pro golfer who was involved in designing a golf course at a new resort; Patachou, the French chanteuse appearing at another local hotel; and Rita Moreno, who was on the island to judge the Miss USA beauty contest.

And then I quit.

I had no idea what I would do next.

It was an impulsive decision. I had worked as a journalist for 17 years without ever analyzing why. I suddenly admitted to myself that it was not the right field for me at all; I had the opposite of the personality required. I had found my niche in light feature stories and rarely had to deal with "hard news" or the people who made it. Still, interviews are the principle source of info for any story and as a very private and shy person I found it very difficult to pry into personal lives, to ask the probing questions that would reveal the terrific story. I always knew I had just skimmed the surface. And writing under pressure was stressful for me. Each story was a struggle, and looming deadlines were a nightmare.

I had become a journalist because of my father. He would have liked to be one and he encouraged me in that direction. Although he was long dead when it came time for me to go to work, I think I followed his wishes because I still wanted to please him. I never considered another career.

I didn't realize what a toll it took on me until I was well out of it, when I was plagued by anxiety dreams about getting the story, asking the questions and meeting the deadlines. The dreams lasted for 15 years! I never wanted to write again, and I didn't until the late '80s.

Living in San Juan

In the six years I lived in San Juan I studied Spanish all the time--group classes or private lessons. I learned to read the language fairly well and could even write it a bit but never got good at understanding the spoken word and I was terrible at speaking it.

Now I admit I'm hopeless at all languages and don't even try to learn. In Puerto Rico I was lucky because when I was there in the 60s most people spoke and understood at least some English so I didn't really need to learn Spanish. (Now it apparently isn't taught in schools except as a second language so English speakers are almost rare.)

I felt comfortable living in San Juan and lived in a variety of neighborhoods. I moved several times. When I lived in New York I stayed put residentially but changed jobs very often. In San Juan, once I got the job on the *Star* there was nowhere else for me to work so my restlessness took the form of changing living quarters. My salary was half what I had made in New York but luckily the rents were also much less than there.

I started in a *casita*, a nice little efficiency cottage behind a doctor's house in a nice neighborhood. Then I made a bad move to a larger apartment in a worse neighborhood. My mother came to visit and was so appalled at my surroundings she offered to pay half the price of renting a condo, so I moved.

An art teacher lived and had a studio in that building and I took a series of her oil painting classes. She taught in a very much hands-on style, so in no time I thought I was creating quite wonderful paintings. Soon I realized they were more hers than mine, but at least she left a spark I later re-kindled.

Then I moved on to my new job at the *Star* and a new home in a more affordable apartment complex in a commercial area. It was a duplex on the seventh and eighth floors. I loved the small balcony where I was sometimes in the clouds overlooking tree tops.

I had been trying to stop smoking for many years. Here I finally succeeded. There was an Olympic-size swimming pool on the property, open till 9 PM. I dove in every day after work, often in the dark, and swam laps. Somehow this helped get me over the addiction hump. I started cooking good dinners for myself and for the first time in years gained some weight. Painfully angular all my life, I finally filled out to a degree I considered downright voluptuous.

My personality changed from Type A to Type B. I went from hyper and stressed to more relaxed and cool, from a night owl to an early riser. It was a very welcome transformation and seemed to happen almost overnight.

My idol at the moment was Paul Newman and a large poster of him—black and white with blue eyes-- graced the top of the stairs. A warning to anyone nearing my bedroom of my high standards.

My boyfriends ranged from a tall, dark and handsome Argentinian journalist/cartoonist to a blond executive in an oil company. I also had an artist admirer who filled my walls with his paintings. The art work but not the artist moved with me to my final apartment in the Condado, the tourist area, where for the first time I could see a sliver of the ocean if I stood exactly here and looked just there.

Before I left the duplex I took a vacation on a Windjammer Barefoot Cruise. I had done very little sailing in my life but this suddenly appealed: an old wooden schooner that offered cheap rides "down island" (south in the island chain) with like-minded passengers. "Barefoot" is a positive word in my vocabulary.

It was a great vacation. For one who had traveled a lot alone and never talked to anyone in airplanes, hotels or restaurants, this setting was perfect. A small group, mostly young, mingling easily. I drank with the passengers and smoked pot with the crew.

I was not much of a pot smoker. I was too old to be a hippie (I was in my 30s in the 60s but I did cover my white VW Beetle with flower power stickers) and, once I finally managed to stop smoking tobacco I was afraid that smoking anything would start me off again. Also, by the time the pot came out at parties I had usually had a lot to drink and knew enough to not mix the two. Only once did I make that mistake. My dear hostess put me to bed in her kids' room. When I awoke early the next morning, I sneaked out of her house and drove home and had a long humiliating walk to the elevator in my long party dress, carrying my wig.

Wig? Yes. My short, almost-black hair was absolutely straight and since I didn't want to go to a beauty parlor every week to have it improved (in those days a matter of rollers and half an hour under a dryer) I had a couple of wigs for special occasions. One of them looked just like my hair only nicer, the other was shoulder length and streaked blond, for when I chose to be incognito, like going to a concert without a date.

My move to the new apartment was good for my social life because I lived much closer to some people I really liked and spent a lot more time with them. Queenie (Irene) Cerqueira and Betty Fairbank were co-owners of a real estate firm. I had done a feature on them for the STAR Magazine and they subsequently became good friends.

Queenie was the warmest, most convivial person I've ever known. Everyone in San Juan loved her. When she and I took a trip to Greece together I was amazed to find that everyone in Greece loved her too! She had an easy way of making everyone, including the elderly woman selling soup on the sidewalk, feel like her best friend. She certainly was mine! Her partner of many years was Don, a gorgeous banker. They were good friends of Betty and her husband Jim, a successful businessman. I was lucky to be embraced by this quartet and the Fairbanks' two teenage daughters, Susie and K-Kin (Carolyn), who are still good friends today.

Me partying at the Fairbanks' condo in San Juan.

Jim had a small plane—a four-seater Cessna. I was a white-knuckle flyer but when the Fairbanks invited me to fly to Ponce, on the south shore, one Sunday morning I said yes. Jim, Betty, their daughter Susie and I took off. Susie was at the "wheel"! Learning to fly! That made me apprehensive, to say the least, but all the Fairbanks seemed cool so I tried to be too. However, when I saw Susie nodding off I felt it was prudent to point that out. Jim casually pinched her awake and we continued on.

Puerto Rico is beautiful to fly over, all country and hills in the middle. When we got to the south coast we first landed on a beach! For fun I guess! Then took off again and landed at the Ponce airport. We stretched our legs, walked around a bit, got a snack, got back in the plane and flew back to San Juan. When I went to work the next day and someone asked "What did you do this weekend?" I enjoyed responding: "Flew to Ponce for a coke."

The Fairbanks also had a large beautiful sailboat, *Fiddler's Green* (named for the mythical sailor's heaven), a 52-foot ketch Jim built, the last in a long series of boats he built himself. I was invited to join them for weekend sails.

It's a fairly long sail from the San Juan Yacht Club, where they kept the boat, to the eastern end of Puerto Rico. The destination was always way beyond that, to off-shore islands.

Culebra was the closest but was usually inundated with "the Spanish Armada" or the "Puerto Rican Navy", the nicknames for the many huge motor boats that Puerto Ricans play in every weekend. (Vieques is the other nearby island now considered part of the "Spanish Virgin Islands" but at that time it was still being used by the U.S Navy for bombing practice.)

So the goal was usually to reach the Virgin Islands—U.S. or British. We took off Friday after work and sailed overnight to St. Thomas (USVI) or Tortola (BVI). This could be a rough trip, into the wind. We wanted to be back in the San Juan Yacht Club by Sunday evening so that left us just Saturday to explore these great cruising grounds. We made the most of it, island hopping, swimming and snorkeling, eating and drinking. Queenie often mooned other yachts as they passed by. Jim brought his guitar and we ended most evenings singing along to old favorites.

Jim had always dreamed of leaving his boat on a mooring in the BVI and flying over for weekends. The flight would take just an hour or so and the rest of the time they could be enjoying leisurely sailing. But he didn't want to leave his valuable yacht unattended.

When I quit my job at the *Star* and was hanging around wondering what to do next the Fairbanks proposed that I live on their boat in Tortola. They knew that I knew nothing about boats; my only contribution to our sails together had been making the Bloody Marys! But they were convinced this would be a win-win deal. They could pop over whenever they felt like it and I would have something to do. I agreed to do it for two months. Who knew this was to become a turning point in my life and I'd still be in Tortola eight years later!

III
MY BOAT YEARS
1972-1985

The Caribbean

On Labor Day weekend, 1972, the *Fiddler's Green* set sail from San Juan, Puerto Rico, to Tortola in the British Virgin Islands. Aboard were Jim Fairbank, the owner and builder of the boat, his wife Betty, our friends Queenie and Don and me.

Jim had put down a mooring in Maya Cove, a small anchorage behind a reef on the east end of the island where the charter company Caribbean Sailing Yachts (CSY) was located. He intended to leave his 52-foot ketch there indefinitely, with me aboard as the "boat sitter".

I had quit my job at the *San Juan Star* and didn't know what to do next. They had always wanted to keep their boat in the BVIs, where the sailing is spectacular. Even though I knew nothing about boats, they invited me to boat-sit and I said sure. We were all a bit happy-go-lucky then.

As soon as we arrived Jim invited the entire CSY crew and everyone anchored in the cove aboard for cocktails. Everyone came-- several tanned and toned young men, a couple of wives and girlfriends, and a few local guys. They all stayed and stayed, and we finally made an impromptu meal out of whatever we had aboard. From then on, the *Green* was an accepted part of the community.

The next day I got a crash course in boat maintenance: how and when to start the engine to charge the batteries that gave me lights and a freezer/ice box; how to catch rain water on the awning and get it into the water tanks; how to light an alcohol stove and how to run the outboard motor on the dinghy so that I could get ashore; it was too big to row.

My delivery crew flew back to San Juan and I was on my own, responsible for a valuable yacht. That was never a problem, as I was surrounded by men who were knowledgeable about boats and were eager to help me out. I had unwittingly fallen into a scenario where I was the only unattached female in a pack of unattached men.

Thanks to CSY, there was always something to do. A thatch-roofed hut on the shore front was the hangout, the Bilge Bar. Any liquor that came off the charter boats was put there for common consumption. When the crew knocked off work at 4:30 they congregated there, and those of us living on boats in the cove came ashore to join them for free drinks. Once a week we piled into a company Land Rover to go to town for pizza. There were parties at houses in the neighborhood or on private boats.

I had arrived with my little portable typewriter and paper and a watercolor pad and paints, thinking I would write or paint some every day. Hah! I don't think I ever pulled out either.

Fiddler's Green **under sail in the BVI.**

My first visitor was my friend Deirdre, the secretary in Queenie and Betty's real estate firm. We were in hysterics all weekend, as I was still having trouble navigating the dingy and often ended up in the mangroves when I tried to get to the dock. I hadn't mastered the alcohol stove and we spent hours cooking a chicken in the oven

The Fairbanks and their guests flew over at least one weekend a month, when we cruised and partied through the other islands of the BVI. They brought most of the food. I contributed duty-free booze. Before each visit I went to Roadtown to stock up on liquor and wine and whatever staples we needed. I loved Main Street, a sweet little winding lane with mostly small houses serving as stores. (It's now hard to find as "town" is now big buildings on filled land.)

To get to town, several miles away, I bummed rides from CSY crew. To get home with all my shopping I hitch-hiked or took a taxi. (I later bought a two-piece bike from Taiwan which I rode into the village of East End for in-between shopping.)

I had been in the cove a few months when I went to Connecticut for Christmas with my family. When I came back there was a new boat in the cove, *Solanderi*, a powder blue catamaran, with an English guy and a French woman aboard. The woman left shortly after and the guy, Peter Hansen, started going ashore evenings, but only occasionally. I liked his looks and I liked his reserve. I was tiring of the constant partying and many nights chose not to go ashore but stayed aboard reading. Peter and I soon got together at a Bilge Bar party. We danced and were almost immediately a couple.

I had run out of birth control pills and during the month or so I waited for Queenie to bring me more Peter and I had time to get to know and like each other. By the time we were able to have sex we felt like soul mates. We shared a childish, playful attitude and once, while "stealing" coconuts ashore, we both said—simultaneously—"I don't ever want to grow up." I took that as a sign that we were meant to be together. Books were another bond. He told me he was attracted to me when he saw me reading aboard rather than partying ashore. When I first went aboard his boat I was pleased to see that he had plenty of books.

His boat was a Wharram catamaran, a very basic Do It Yourself vessel designed by a Welshman, James Wharram. Peter had been living and working on a tug boat in the Mediterranean when he found *Solanderi* for sale at a low-low price he could manage and decided that he would buy it and sail around the world. He found a couple of young men willing to learn-as-you-go and that was his crew for the trans-Atlantic crossing. They arrived in Barbados without incident.

But *en route* up the island chain a cross-beam had broken. Peter's intention was to hole up in Maya Cove for a while, take down his mast, replace the crossbeam and do a lot of other work before continuing on to the Pacific. How lucky for him that I had a comfortable yacht for him to eat and sleep on! He worked on his boat all day, with a break for lunch and a "siesta" on *Fiddlers Green*. It was too hot to make love below decks at midday so we made ourselves an airy boudoir on the cabin top where the large awning hid us from passers-by. In the evenings we usually went ashore for showers and a couple of drinks, then I cooked dinner for us on the *Green*.

For the first time in my life I was wifely, preparing three meals a day for my man. It was quite a job, as I had never been much of a cook and Peter had a huge appetite. He stayed skinny as a rail. I put on some weight, which I needed.

Our little family also included a dog, Mister Wags, who had sailed from England with Peter. He was a medium sized brown and white collie mix, perfectly trained. He went everywhere with Peter and did exactly as he was told. Peter didn't own a leash. He said "Mind your manners" and the dog did. Peter took him ashore for nice long "walkies" every morning and evening.

Peter, Mr. Wags and me on *Solanderi*.

Peter's plan was to work his way around the world. When he arrived in Tortola he was practically penniless. His few clothes were close to rags. His supplies were down to a few cans of food. But ever confident and resourceful, and naturally skilled at most things having any connection with boats, he was soon picking up odd jobs at CSY to make a little money. Very soon he was occasionally skippering a charter boat. His very first gig as a charter captain was for two couples from Boston who became immediate friends. They invited Mr. Wags and me to join them for their week of sailing in the BVIs and when we were later in Massachusetts we went sailing on their boat.

Meanwhile, Peter's beam job dragged on and on, which was fine with me; he wasn't going to leave for a while. When it was finally finished we took a brief shake-down cruise to St. Maarten with a couple from another British boat in Maya Cove. It was my first ocean passage and, though I didn't know it then, the Anegada Passage is known as one of the roughest in the area. We apparently hit extra rough weather, as it took us 36 hours rather than the usual 24.

I didn't own foul weather gear; I didn't even know what it was. I stayed below most of the time to keep dry, but whenever I poked my head up I saw a frightening scene, like Peter and Brian wrestling the jib down on the pitching deck. I wondered if we would make it and was surprised to find when it was all over that the experienced sailors thought nothing of it, considered it a fairly routine passage. Sailing back from St. Maarten I could see why people enjoyed cruising. We had a lovely calm and speedy return in perfect conditions.

Barbara, a college friend, and her 16-year-old daughter, another Deirdre, my godchild, came to visit me. It was my first glimpse of them since Deirdre's christening—that's what a dedicated godparent I was! And that's when Peter realized I was 6½ years older than he. I looked much younger than I was then, and it was quite a blow to him. He turned all quiet and thoughtful and I was afraid I would lose him. But he bounced right back within a day and our age difference never seemed to matter ever again.

Our lives fell into a pleasant routine. In between Peter's odd jobs for CSY and others, we sailed *Solanderi* around the BVIs, discovering shallow anchorages where we, with only three-foot draft, could go but most boats couldn't. (In those days catamarans were rare; now they are more popular than monohulls.)

Peter's boat, *Solanderi*, under sail in the BVI.

There was a congenial group coming and going in Maya Cove. Most of the men worked ashore for CSY and the women worked on their boats. The Fairbanks and friends continued to come about monthly. I always went sailing with them, and Peter eventually came with us too.

Despite my new love, I was still insecure and could often show it. I could be moody, hurt, jealous or just plain unhappy. Luckily Peter turned out to be the only person I ever encountered who knew instinctively how to get me out of it, either ignoring me, teasing me or somehow letting me know he cared. I felt secure enough to let love blossom. And I really liked him. He had none of the hang-ups most people in my previous life had. He was a happy, cheerful guy, doing what he wanted to do, which was simply to live on his boat and sail around the world.

He treated everyone well. An early lesson I learned from him was Give a smile, Get a smile. I would approach sales clerks in what I now call New Yorker mode (totally tuned out to their humanity), then complain that they were surly and uncooperative. He treated everyone as a fellow human being and in his quiet way got whatever service he wanted. I'm ashamed to admit I didn't know any better, but I learned from Peter's example and felt I became a much nicer person thanks to him.

Eventually Peter was ready to move on. But before heading for the Pacific he wanted to see a bit of the United States and planned to cruise through the Bahamas *en route*. He asked me to go with him. I was hesitant about sailing up the east coast, afraid of the open ocean, so he agreed to take the IW (Intracoastal Waterway). I could certainly handle that.

I hated to break the news to the Fairbanks that I was leaving the *Green* and sailing away with Peter, but I had lasted much longer than any of us had dreamed, about a year and a half. I think they were very surprised that I was giving up the comfortable *Green* for *Solanderi*, which had no electricity, no refrigerator, no shower, no diesel engine, no comfortable cockpit or bunks. It was a very basic floating bachelor pad. They couldn't believe that I was that serious about a boat bum. But rather than making other plans for the *Green*, they sold her.

Solanderi

Peter knew his boat wasn't suitable for a woman and was eager to make it more attractive. We scrubbed the interior clean and he cleared out unneeded junk. He scraped and sanded everything and I painted and varnished. He upgraded his outboard motor from a seven horsepower putt-putt to a monstrous 50-horsepower thing he put together out of used parts. He remade some hand-me-down sails. He made new, lockable hatch covers before we got to the big city, San Juan.

There we had fun with my old friends from the six years I had lived there. We took a boatload of them on a harbor cruise to show off the boat. We bought foam cushions and vinyl from which we made cushion covers and I sewed curtains. Peter loved Puerto Rico and the people. I appreciated it again seeing it through his eyes. Then we finally got underway for what I called Honeymoon Cruise #1.

The Mona Passage between Puerto Rico and the Dominican Republic is notoriously rough. The first time we tried it we blew out both the main and mizzen sails. We tacked back to Puerto Rico with just the jib and engine in the dark with winds howling and seas crashing.

I was terrified and I felt so sorry for Peter; it seemed to me his world and his dream were being destroyed. Not at all. We spent a couple of days repairing the sails, then tried again.

We made it and then for the next few days I was learning that cruising seemed to be at least one scary adventure a day interspersed with delightful interludes.

There's an adage: Cruising is hours of pure boredom punctuated by moments of sheer terror. I loved the "boring" hours, when nothing happened, and hated the terrifying moments, which included dragging anchors, running aground, hitting coral heads, thunderstorms, engine quitting, things breaking, sails ripping. There were far too many adversities, yet I kept going. Obviously, I really loved the guy.

My journal entry after the aborted Mona Passage crossing says for the first time it occurred to me that one or both of us could drown. Yet Peter proved over and over that no matter how horrendous the situation looked to me he could get us out of it safely. I guess I figured he was worth whatever it took.

Me steering *Solanderi* on a good day.

From the Dominican Republic we headed north to the Turks and Caicos Islands and then island-hopped through the Bahamas, snorkeling, trying unsuccessfully to catch fish with line and spear, enjoying the little villages and friendly natives and local bread, meeting a few other yachts but not a lot of them, disliking tourist developments, which seemed so artificial compared to the "real" places. We had left Tortola in mid-April and arrived in Miami on the Fourth of July. We got haircuts and I bought clothes.

Our ultimate destination in the U.S. was New England, where my family and Peter could meet each other. True to his word, Peter started up the IW from Miami.

It was not much fun—hot and buggy and our boat wasn't made for motoring. We sailed when we could but at every bridge we had to take down sails, turn on the engine and circle the unwieldy catamaran in crowded quarters until the bridge opened.

We had a nice couple of days with my old New York roommate Pat and her family in Port St. Lucie. Pat insisted we borrow her car to go to Disney World, so we did, and enjoyed it a lot. Then we went to Kennedy Space Center and loved that too.

Back on the IW, there were violent thunder storms late every afternoon, just as we were looking for a place to anchor overnight. By the time we got to the northern end of Florida, which was smelly as well as hot and buggy, even I was ready to go to sea. Peter was greatly relieved to get out from the confined waterway.

We made one return to shore to see Charleston, where we met a bunch of people who wined and dined us, took us shopping, let us use washers and dryers, etc. I was learning that cruisers are often treated with considerable interest and hospitality.

Back out to sea we ran into strong northeasterly winds off of Cape Fear. After beating our brains out going nowhere for three days, I finally mutinied. Peter acquiesced surprisingly easily and we headed for the nearest channel into the intracoastal, Southport, NC. There, in another surprising move, we went to a marina and rented a slip for a couple of months. Peter had never before paid money for a place to keep the boat. We bought an old car and continued our northward journey by road.

We stopped at the Connecticut shore, where my brother Tom and his family were camping, then went to Martha's Vineyard, where my mother was staying with her friend Ginny. The dear old ladies were in a dither I'm sure over sleeping arrangements but they very coolly turned over the entire upstairs to us. That way they weren't condoning our sleeping together but if we were doing it they didn't have to know.

Back in Southport, we worked on the boat until hurricane season was over. Peter made a self-steering vane and installed a head (toilet) in the starboard cabin, replacing the one in a cramped airless locker which was accessed from the deck. He also made it possible to have a shower below deck when necessary. Most of the time we bathed in the sea and rinsed off with fresh water on deck but there were times when we needed another option. He also made a new mainsail.

We met Bill, a young man who had a small Wharram cat (the same design as *Solanderi*) which he sailed around the area. We signed him up to make the passage back to Tortola with us. It was to be my first passage of more than one night and I was afraid I wouldn't be good crew, that I'd be sick or afraid or sleepy, generally inadequate. Peter's plan was to go east, then south, as directly as possible, no stops this time.

It was a 10-day passage with delightful days alternating with rough and scary days. When I lay in my bunk I could feel the plywood sides flex with each crashing wave and I wondered how much of that the boat could take before bursting.

But Peter treated it all as routine and expected me to perform, so I did. I was able to stand my watches, prepare three meals a day and take care of Bill, who got seasick right away and stayed in his bunk for three or four days.

I was ecstatic about the self-steering vane. Up till then one of us had to be at the helm all the time. Now the vane steered the boat. Whoever was on watch could go about his business anywhere on the boat and just check the compass and the sails periodically.

Back in Tortola, Peter had plenty of work all winter skippering for various charter companies and working on the boats at CSY. We had been together two years now, an all-time record for me. Since my one long-term boyfriend in college I had never had a relationship that lasted more than six months.

In June we flew from there to England to spend a couple of weeks with Peter's parents, who were then living in Wokingham, near London. I guess I passed inspection because from then on his father signed cards to me with "Love, Dad".

We then spent about six months "down island", along the Lesser Antilles chain. In St. Marten we picked up a small propane fridge we had ordered from Holland (yay—what luxury!) and then had a very close call with Hurricane Eloise.

Queenie and Don had come to visit. After enjoying St. Barts and Saba we sailed back to Simpson Bay where we anchored between two reefs, having no idea a hurricane was on the way. We had a wild night, with torrential rain and the boat lurching as if we were at sea. We were very lucky. The anchor held. In Philipsburg harbor not far from us at least two boats were washed up on the shore. Never again were we lax about checking the weather forecasts.

In the spring of 1976, after helping deliver a friend's boat from England to Tortola, Peter started a job with regular hours at CSY, a major digression for this free spirit. He agreed to stay for a year. He was Boat Supervisor.

We bought a VW Beetle painted metallic blue, which I later totaled. I was driving into town when I reached into my bag for something. Next thing I was off the road with the windshield in my face and the steering column in my knees. Passersby helped me out of the car and took me to the hospital, where I needed a few stitches next to my eye. That's all.

I was drinking two or three Bloody Marys every morning at that time, but it never occurred to me the accident could have been alcohol-related. Only rarely did I admit to myself I had had too much to drink, and that was usually at the end of the day, if there was a party.

And Peter never mentioned my drinking, never indicated he thought I had a problem or that he was embarrassed by my behavior. In fact it was obvious he liked me best when I was high; I lost my inhibitions and was more fun. Unintentionally, he was an enabler.

I kept a buzz on most of the time, starting with Bloody Marys, going on to wine and/or vodka. I still kept Canadian Club, my pre-boat drink, on hand for when I really "needed" a drink.

For a long time I had waking and sleeping dreams about my accident, about what could have happened. When I drove off the road I hit a tree that stopped me from falling down a cliff to the sea.

Peter's job stretched to two years. The company moved from Maya Cove to Baugher's Bay in Roadtown Harbour. We eventually moved *Solanderi* there too.

Maya Cove had been an idyllic anchorage, pretty, protected by a reef, clean, off the charter boat route and with just a few private boats anchored out.

Baugher's Bay was not pretty and was an open roadstead. The boat rocked and rolled a lot. So in the summers we moved our home to Cane Garden Bay at the west end of the island and Peter commuted by car from there.

That was another idyllic anchorage, much bigger than Maya Cove, with a lovely big crescent beach rising to mountains. There were a couple of funky local bars on the beach and only a few boats anchored. Now I hear the beach is all built up and the boats are packed in.

I don't know what I did with myself those two years Peter worked fulltime for CSY. I stupidly never kept a journal when we were in port for a long time, only when we were cruising. I worked on the boat of course. That was endless. I wasn't writing or painting. I played tennis once in a while.

I enjoyed my little sailing dingy. I had bought my own dinghy early on because I never wanted to be dependent on anyone else for transportation. It was a sweet little sailing dingy but I usually rowed it. The first time I tried sailing it I took Mr. Wags with me and managed to knock him overboard when I jibed!

We had a lot of friends, mostly other cruisers or people working with charter yachts, and we were all quite sociable. We sailed to other islands some weekends. The San Juan gang still came over now and then and we went there. My nephew John came to visit twice, when he was 13 and 15 I think. He learned a bit about sailing and now lives on the Connecticut shore with easy access to boats and sailing clubs. We did a little house-sitting, which I really enjoyed. Peter's family came to visit—Mum, Dad and niece Chrissie.

I went to Connecticut probably a couple of times a year, more if Mum had a medical crisis.

Her health was scary. In addition to osteoporosis, which caused her pain for many years, she had two emergency surgeries for blockages in her intestines, she had a broken hip, she had pneumonia and malnutrition. I worried about her a lot but as long as I was in the Caribbean I felt I could get to her quickly enough if needed. I didn't know what I'd do when Peter was ready to go to the Pacific, whether I could/should go that far away from her.

In February, 1979, we had a series of going away parties, then set off on a Caribbean circle tour, possibly never to return to Tortola—or the Caribbean. We visited just about every island in the sea and on the shorelines of all the South and Central American countries bordering on the Caribbean except for Colombia, which was considered too dangerous then. We ended in Tampa, Florida, where CSY had headquarters and made the boats.

Most of the passages were rough and unpleasant and I wondered at times whether I could keep doing them. Many of the anchorages were not safe (weather-wise) and not pleasant. The formalities of customs and immigration at each island were a time-consuming hassle.

And yet every new place was eagerly anticipated and usually enjoyed. We usually met other yachties and often had nice encounters with locals ashore. I always had food shopping to do—bread and fresh fruit and veggies-- and we usually had at least one meal out. We collected mail and sent mail. I called Mum. We explored by foot or boat or dinghy. Only rarely did we rent a car or take a taxi and that was only if I insisted.

On the outskirts of Tampa we found a nice protected spot to anchor off a friendly little yacht club. Peter made all new cross-beams for the boat—again! We also spruced up the living area. Since we were usually in the tropics where the weather was lovely and warm, we lived on deck most of the time. *Solanderi* had a nice big center deck between the hulls, about 10 feet square, where we ate and spent most of our leisure time and, when in port, slept. Peter replaced the slatted deck with a solid one, put a slatted bench on either side where we put cushions and pillows when in port. We pulled these into the center deck at night to make our double bed.

Our home afloat: 1. On deck: our living/dining/bedroom. 2. Our bunk.
3. The galley. 4. The "salon", also our navigation table.

When finished we crossed Florida on the Okeechobee Waterway, my only experience sailing in fog. Don met us on the east coast and he and Peter sailed *Solanderi* back to San Juan, where we were to make our final preparations for the Pacific—finally! I went to Connecticut to say goodbye to my family.

The Pacific Ocean
1980-1985

In March, 1980, we finally set sail for the Pacific, where we spent the next five years. Mum's health was OK when we left and, miraculously, she stayed healthy the whole time I was far away. I didn't have to feel guilty about abandoning her when she needed me. I worried only about her worrying about me.

I knew she was chronically worried about me being at sea but I'm grateful that she didn't let me know the extent of her agony until after it was all over. If I had known I might have felt I had to give up the cruising life as intolerable cruelty to her. She could have manipulated me, as she often had done in the past. I'm surprised and so thankful that she didn't. She must have loved me a lot to let my love for Peter take me where it would. And she lived through it.

The Pacific years were fabulous, with a story book quality unlike anything we found in the more familiar Caribbean. Big chunks of our time were spent in New Zealand (six months), Australia (1 ½ years) and Guam (one year), but it's the islands of Polynesia, Melanesia and Micronesia that are most memorable, because they were so foreign.

The most striking common denominator was effusive hospitality, a far cry from the reticence or indifference we often found in the Caribbean.

My theory is that because the Pacific Islanders were indigenous they were comfortable as hosts. Their people had always been hospitable and they carried on the heritage. Their ancestors had lived through years of colonialism yet, except for accepting Christianity, they had more or less kept their culture intact.

The so-called West Indians who dominate the Caribbean, on the other hand, are descended from African slaves. Their attitude toward white men is understandably more complex and not necessarily so welcoming.

I say white men because with one exception the cruisers I met were all white. We met only one black American man, who was cruising solo in the Pacific.

The Pacific Ocean is divided into three geographical areas. Polynesia covers a huge area from Hawaii above the equator to New Zealand way below. The western part of the Pacific is made up of Melanesia below the equator and Micronesia above.

In my log I have written that "Micronesia means tiny islands, Polynesia means many islands and Melanesia means black islands". I don't know who made these distinctions or why, but we definitely noticed a physical difference in the inhabitants of each group. In general the Polynesians are brown, short and stocky, the Melanesians black, tall and thin, and the Micronesians are tan and smaller with slightly Asian features.

Most of them were very welcoming to cruising yachts when we were there in the early 80s, especially on the more remote islands, where we were rare indeed.

We crossed most of the Pacific, about 8000 miles, in the first seven months. We would have enjoyed more time in many of the islands we visited, but as always when sailing in the tropics, we had cyclone season on our minds.

In the southern hemisphere the cyclone season is December-May, the opposite of the northern hurricane season. We entered the Pacific in April, 1980, and wanted to be in New Zealand, out of the cyclone belt, by November. That meant we cruised at a fairly fast pace through all of Polynesia and some of Melanesia but we still managed to see most of the islands en route.

Polynesia

We made the 4000 mile passage from the Panama Canal to the Marquesa Islands in French Polynesia in 35 days, with our good friend Don as crew. Our landfall was Hiva Oa, and from there we cruised through the rest of the Marquesas, some of the Tuamoto atolls and all the Society Islands, the three groups that make up French Polynesia.

Queenie, my best friend and Don's girlfriend, joined us in Tahiti, which we found quite westernized, and the four of us went on together to explore the other Society Islands.

Moorea turned out to be my favorite island in the whole Pacific, one where I thought I could live. My journal exclaims about "gorgeous green hills and mountains, beautiful beaches, a barrier reef completely surrounding the island and a fabulous turquoise lagoon with lovely swimming and snorkeling." I even loved the houses, mostly with bamboo walls and palm thatch roofs, surrounded by beautiful flowers and shrubs. And I loved the wine and cheese.

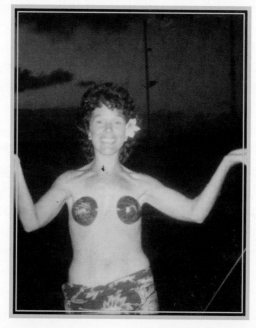

Our friend Queenie wearing coconut shell bra made by Peter.

We also loved Bora-Bora, where we joined the Bastille Day festivities and Peter, inspired by the *tamure* dancers' costumes, made a coconut shell bra for Queenie.

She and Don left us there to return to their lives in Puerto Rico. We sailed on westward.

In the Cook Islands-- once British, then a protectorate of New Zealand, now independent— we stopped by tiny privately-owned Palmerston Atoll, which is populated entirely by the descendants of one William Marsters, an Englishman, and his three Polynesian wives. When we were there 76 Marsters were in residence. We met all of them, it seemed, and at least half of them came aboard *Solanderi* for a short sail.

American Samoa is one of three island groups in the Pacific still under American rule. It's hard to believe but the USA, "the land of the free," is just about the only remaining colonial power in both the Caribbean and Pacific oceans.

The other American "territories" in the Pacific are Guam and the Federated States of Micronesia, which we would visit later. There are two in the Caribbean: Puerto Rico and the U.S. Virgin Islands (my former and present homes).They were all acquired for military reasons.

A rarely known fact is that we residents are all second-class citizens of the US. We cannot vote for our president and we have no representation in Congress except for a "delegate" who can sit on committees but cannot vote.

Pago Pago (pronounced Pango), the capital of American Samoa, was a big disappointment. Its magnificent big harbor had been polluted by a huge fleet of Korean fishing boats and tuna canning factories. It's also the only place we saw litter.

From Samoa we crossed the dateline and entered The Kingdom of Tonga, where royalty still rules a large group of islands which was declared a constitutional monarchy in the 19th century by an ambitious chief. It's probably the only island group in the Pacific that has never been colonized and they seemed to be doing quite well for themselves.

They were very friendly and hospitable and made a variety of very good crafts. We "bought" baskets and mats, tapa cloth made from pounded bark and two adorable small grass skirts. We planned to be in New Zealand by Christmas time where we would meet up with Tortola friends who had two little girls about that size.

This was the beginning of our "trading" territory. In the more remote islands there isn't much use for money but there is a need for goods. Instead of paying for our purchases with cash, we were stocked with a lot of trading goods, everything from rice to kerosene to jeans and needle and thread,

From there we hurried on to Fiji, spending a couple of weeks in the capital of Suva, a large city and quite civilized, preparing for our passage to New Zealand. We planned to return to Fiji after the cyclone season and do some leisurely cruising in the outer islands then. We had a young man aboard as crew, an American who was bicycling his way around the world, hitch-hiking free rides between land masses with cruisers like us.

New Zealand

New Zealand was our home for about six months, the duration of the cyclone season. Our home port was in the Bay of Islands on the northern tip of the North Island. We were anchored off Russell, the main town, with several other cruising yachts, many of whom we already knew, others who were soon friends, so we had an active social life.

Peter and most of the other guys and many of the "girls" found jobs ashore, especially during the high tourist season, December and January (their summer). I mostly stayed on the boat painting, varnishing and sewing.

Peter worked as a mechanic at a gas station and found a junked car he resurrected so that we could take a road trip. Then we spent about a month touring both the north and south islands. Christchurch was the only town we liked but we found the countryside absolutely beautiful almost everywhere we went.

Miles of fertile farm and ranch land cover gentle hills now and then interrupted by lovely lakes. I loved the millions of white fluffy sheep we encountered and the "shepherds" that rounded them up-- farmers on horseback or motorcycles! Each was attended by at least one dog; traditional Border Collies were vastly outnumbered by mutts of all varieties.

The South Island was so unique and spectacular even Peter was willing to do all the touristy things: a boat ride through Milford Sound, a fiord from which tall steep mountains rise and waterfalls crash down; a plane ride over glaciers where we could see deep crevices that were a lovely pale blue.

Peter had made a plywood sleeping platform for the back of our van but we rarely used it once we discovered that the Kiwis really cater to budget travelers. For a few dollars a night we could rent a little cabin with beds, a table and chairs and sometimes a kitchenette. If there wasn't a kitchenette there was a central kitchen near the communal toilets and shower, TV room and laundry facility. We dried our wet laundry on the roadside when we stopped to make our sandwiches for lunch.

We were not shoppers so rarely cruised the stores but, knowing we were going to spend a year in Australia, I decided to knit myself a sweater with the lovely soft New Zealand homespun sheep wool. I found a pattern for a sweater/jacket with nice designs and pockets and bought great shades of brown, tan, gray and white. I hadn't knitted for years and had never done anything as complicated as a jacket but figured I was up to it and it would help pass the time on long night watches. I was, it did, and the completed garment was actually attractive and wonderfully cozy.

We happened to be passing through Auckland when Prince Charles happened to be making a visit there. I was on the street with camera ready and got an unobstructed close-up of the waving prince, who was quite young then, as he drove by. Unfortunately I had not advanced the film so didn't get my shot.

When we were there in 1981 the idyllic-seeming country wasn't doing that well. The Socialist government provided free education and health care but enterprise was so highly taxed that many found it impossible to get ahead and were leaving for Australia.

The indigenous Maoris, who were admired for their customs in the tourist areas, were definitely second class citizens in other places where, along with many immigrants from other Polynesian islands, they seemed to be mostly drunken bums.

I wrote in my journal "It was a real shocker. We were so used to the gentle, easy-going, friendly, industrious, creative islanders that I was unprepared for the loss of dignity." I also thought the pubs were disgusting.

However, back in the Bay of Islands, I loved our anchorage and the town where I could dingy ashore and walk to the shops. I felt quite at home there by the time we left, a recognized member of the community, a feeling I hadn't had since I left my home town. I really enjoyed all of New Zealand very much, as much as I could enjoy any place that wasn't tropical.

As soon as the cyclone season was over, we and a lot of other cruising boats hightailed it back to the tropics. Our passage was an uneventful 10 days, some good weather, some bad. (The passage to NZ from Fiji had taken 15 days.) I got a lot of knitting done on my wool jacket.

Two terrible incidents followed later, both concerning boats we had cruised with throughout Polynesia and visited in ports in New Zealand. A big catamaran with a kooky American captain and a crew of fun-loving young people disappeared en route from NZ to Fiji that year, and an historic schooner crewed by several dedicated tall-ship sailors also disappeared some years later somewhere between NZ and Australia.

Stories like these were very sobering in the yachtie community. So were the several books written by survivors of shipwrecks. When you're on a small boat in a big ocean the bogeyman is never far away.

Back in our preferred latitudes, we had only five months to cruise before heading to Australia for the next cyclone season, so we visited only two island groups, Fiji and a bit of Vanuatu. They couldn't have been more different. We revisited both of them again after we left Australia.

Australia

We spent a year and a half in Australia. Peter had been there as a young man looking for adventure, working in the Outback in Alice Springs. There he met a sailor looking for crew back to England and, although he knew nothing about sailing, he signed on. Forever after his life has been all about boats but he was eager to see the country again.

We made landfall in Cairns and expected to spend a lot of time exploring the Great Barrier Reef, but we hadn't done our homework. It's way offshore and there was no place a private boat could anchor. The only way to get there was by tour boat.

Our disappointment didn't last long because stingers (poisonous jelly fish) were everywhere, so we didn't want to go in the water anyway. Instead we checked out all the small towns and big towns on the east coast quite thoroughly, from Cairns to Brisbane, with Peter picking up odd jobs along the way, including helping a young man transform his wrecked trimaran into a serviceable catamaran!

Many of the towns are up a river, including Gladstone, where we ended up spending several months while Peter did major surgery on the boat. The plywood bulwarks had started to rot. He was able to save them by reshaping them, a job that took forever because he was also working fulltime. I called 1982 The Year of the Bulwarks.

We were either anchored in the river or tied to a piling during those months, quite a distance from town. I got a small outboard for my dingy and if Peter was working days I'd meet him at the yacht club for showers, drinks and occasionally a steak dinner.

Yacht clubs, by the way, might sound snooty and be expensive for the locals, but they are heaven for cruising yachts. There seems to be a fairly universal custom of reciprocity among yacht clubs; if you're a member of a yacht club anywhere in the world you're welcome to the use of the local club—for free.

I also bought a small used black and white television set to keep me company when Peter worked nights, sometimes including overtime till 2 AM. His job at an engineering shop was fitter-turner, the trade he had apprenticed for as a young man in England, before he discovered boating.

My trips to town always included a stop at the local library. I looked into Australian authors and found a couple I really liked: the novelist Patrick White, who had won the Nobel Prize for Literature a few years previously (his best-known novel is *The Eye of the Storm*); and A.B. Paterson, a poet also known as The Banjo. A balladeer, really, who wrote mostly about the bush and the men and horses in it. *The Man from Snowy River* is considered his major poem but he's probably best known for *Waltzing Matilda*, the song based on his ballad of that name. The country singer Slim Dusty made it famous—and later we happened to stumble onto a concert where he was playing in the bush! Perfect!

I became a thrift shop devotee while in Gladstone. My journal reminds me: "Little Miss New Yorker that was is now into second-hand clothes. It's such a laugh when I think of Saks and Bonwits and that I wouldn't shop anywhere less. Now I go into an actual store just to look!"

When the bulwarks were finally finished we moved on to Caboolture, near Brisbane, the capital of Queensland, where we put *Solanderi* "on the hard" in a boat yard while we finally went into the Outback.

Again I quote from my diary. "Sometimes we lead a charmed life!" Instead of our usual touring in a beat-up van we could sleep in we had the use of an actual campervan, with a stove and fridge, settee and table, cupboards and sink and running water and a double bed over the cab. But no shower or toilet. It seems Americans are (or were) the only softies who consider these contraptions necessities.

Our vehicle belonged to Nicky and Gaye, a New Zealand couple we had met in Melanesia who were on an extended visit to Oz. They had bought a new bigger van but so far hadn't sold the old one so offered it to us for the duration, then asked if we'd like to join them on a gold-digging expedition! Just what Peter dreamed of!

They were experienced fossickers and had quite a collection of small gold nuggets.

Peter got his fossicking license, bought a used metal detector, and off we went on an adventure that lasted two months.

We travelled miles into the bush, checking out every mullock (debris pile from an old mine) en route in New South Wales and Victoria.

Les had a Eureka find early on—an 8.4 ounce nugget! Over two inches in diameter! The townies in Home Rule had never seen such a nugget—or ever heard of such a find near there.

Unfortunately that bonanza didn't repeat itself ever. Poor Peter, despite days and days of "beeping" in the dirt and hot sun, harassed by biting ants and stinging, clinging flies, never turned up anything but rusty nails, buttons and one horseshoe that didn't bring him any luck.

We moved almost every day, pulling off to the side of the road to camp in the bush and wash in streams. So much nicer than formal camp grounds. We also jumped into public swimming pools whenever we found one. We had over 100-degree days and as we neared the bottom of the continent came into drought areas, experienced one dust storm and drove through the smoke of nearby bush fires.

We ended our search in an area called the Golden Triangle near Melbourne, where Les found his only other nugget, a tiny one, and Peter still found nothing. We parted company there to visit an Englishman who had crewed for Peter on his trans-Atlantic voyage and ended up settling and raising a family near Melbourne.

South of there we witnessed the enchanting Penguin Parade on Philip Island. Fairy Penguins, so-called because they are tiny—13 inches-- surf ashore at dusk after fishing all day. Stuffed with fish for their young, they waddle up the beach and along a road lined with burrows, each bird eventually disappearing into one of them to feed its hungry chicks.

All the wildlife of Australia was delightful. I had always thought koalas looked temptingly cuddly but quickly learned not to hug when I saw the sharp claws. We were able to get up close to all the marsupials: koalas and their smaller and even fluffier kin wombats, kangaroos and their small relatives wallabies. It seemed that every female had an adorable tiny joey in her pouch. I was able to feed a wallaby, whose mouth was gentle and velvety, and a kangaroo.

Me feeding a kangaroo at a park in Australia.

Our road trip continued quite quickly from Melbourne up the east coast. Even Peter, not a city guy, liked Sydney, and we got to sail around the famous harbor with British cruisers we knew from Tortola who were now living there. Back in Queensland, our visas were about to expire and it was time to go cruising again. The boat was still on the hard, where Peter prepared both hulls for new engines.

Because we would later be sailing near the equator, where winds are very light, he realized we needed to upgrade from our old makeshift outboard motor. From the ridiculous to the sublime, he had ordered not one but two diesel engines from Japan. To avoid the steep Australian import tax, which would have doubled the cost, the engines were being shipped to New Caledonia, our next port of call, and we would install them there.

Melanesia

Noumea, the capital of New Caledonia, was advertised as "The Paris of the Pacific." That was a gross exaggeration, though we did enjoy the food and wine of the former French colony and had some good times with the French ex-pats who lived there.

Our twin Japanese engines arrived on time and, with the help of some other yachties, Peter got them secured in *Solanderi*, one in each hull.

This was unaccustomed luxury for us. They certainly changed our M.O. Though Peter would never turn on the engines if he were able to sail, we now could keep going if the wind failed at sea or if it was dangerous to navigate under sail in a tight spot. I could relax more.

When we left there and headed north we were both ecstatic to be back in our chosen milieu, cruising among small idyllic islands, anchoring in calm turquoise bays surrounded by white sandy beaches and swaying coconut palms.

Fiji was my favorite island group in Melanesia. It is also the least typical, the most westernized. Many of the natives we met seemed well-educated and spoke good English, which made it possible for us to have real conversations and to feel at home. It's also one of the biggest and most developed island groups in the western Pacific, and tourism is a fairly big industry so, even though we avoided the resort islands, we were not such rare objects of interest when we arrived at a native village as we were farther north.

In Vanuatu and the Solomon Islands, where we spent the next several months, we were indeed rare. We chose to spend most of our time anchored in quiet bays, which were mostly on outer islands with small villages.

There, the minute we dropped anchor, we were often overwhelmed by many canoes full of mostly young boys, who rushed out to greet us, climbing over our sides, bearing generous gifts of coconuts and fruits, and then sitting down for a long visit.

We had little to welcome such a crowd, just powdered juices and hard candies. We were rarely able to have a conversation —there was sometimes a teacher or bright student who knew some English or French—but that didn't matter to them. They were happy to just look at us, touch us and giggle or shriek with laughter, and to do so for hours!

Peter was naturally gracious and good about coping with the visitors. He would try to make the best of the situation-- learning how to say hello and thank you in their language, showing them what he was working on, showing them magazines. When he ran out of ideas he'd just go about his business, hoping they'd lose interest. They never did! I, a very private person, would eventually disappear below decks, very up-tight about the invasion. Once they got used to our presence, we were allowed some privacy.

They lived communally on the small isolated islands and when we went ashore we were welcomed warmly and always offered food from a communal pot. Most of the outer islands were quite self-sufficient; if they had a "store" it was usually tiny and had little but a few canned goods, maybe some soap and tobacco. Inter-island supply ships, which usually called monthly, brought basics like rice.

We were useful in that we were stocked with things they could use, like kerosene, nails, needle and thread, old T shirts. That's how we reciprocated for gifts and paid for any store supplies, shells or crafts that we bought. They had no use for money.

Many of the crafts here were similar to those in the rest of the Pacific—straw mats etc.—but the carvings were unique. Black ebony wood inlaid with silvery pearl shell designs created a dramatic contrast for objects like human figureheads and food bowls embellished with fish and birds. These were found mostly on the bigger islands with a town, and the sellers realized their value. One paid for a carving with blue jeans.

The islanders we met were the "civilized" ones, descendants of those that the missionaries had Christianized. It's mind-boggling how far and wide their influence has traveled and how successfully they converted their subjects. And it's also amazing that they, the Europeans, were still running many of the churches and schools in many of the places we visited.

We did not meet the "primitive" people who escaped the missionaries, the indigenous tribes, each with its own chief, which still practiced their "heathen" ways. They might live on the same island but they live a totally different lifestyle, up in the hills, in the bush. They had no interest in meeting us.

We couldn't see them in their own villages but we got a good look at a lot of them when they came to Vila, the capital of Vanuatu, for an Independence Day celebration where they took part in the ceremonial dancing. They were all very black. The men were quite fierce looking and were totally naked except for penis sheaths, feathers in the hair and bits of greenery draped over the shoulders.

We started to see debris from the Pacific Theater of World War II. It was mostly scattered—an airplane in the bush here, a sunken boat there—but there was a colossal junkyard on the island of Espiritu Santo in Vanuatu, where most of the inhabitants were living in the old military Quonset huts left behind.

A huge American base had been built there, a city of 100,000 people with 43 movie theaters we were told. When the war was over, the Yanks didn't leave their hosts anything but the huts. Everything that could be moved—every truck and tank—was driven into the sea at the end of the harbor. The beach is littered with rusty hulks; it's called Million Dollar Point.

In the Solomon Islands we saw our only active volcano, a fabulous display of fireworks as we sailed by slowly in the dark. We also had a close encounter with a whale, almost as long as our boat, that we almost ran into while he was sleeping!

And it was there I had my first introduction to betel nuts. The natives chew the nuts and spit out the blood-red juice anywhere they happen to be. This is a custom I find really disgusting.

Papua New Guinea was the most familiar name for me in that part of the world and I expected it to be the most primitive. But it's a huge island group and somehow we went only to islands that were quite westernized, prosperous and modern: Bougainville and New Britain (also the name of my home town in Connecticut). The indigenous tribes were mostly in the highlands elsewhere but I think they are probably quite similar to those we did see in the Solomons and Vanuatu.

In Bougainville we visited the world's largest open-pit copper mine and met a lot of yachties who stopped there for weeks or years to take advantage of the good-paying jobs. In New Britain, the capital of Rabaul was on high alert as a volcano there was considered likely to blow imminently. That was in 1984. Ten years passed before it did erupt, destroying the town.

Micronesia

The Pacific Ocean is so vast that it took us 11 days to sail from PNG to our next destination, the Caroline Islands, now called The Federated States of Micronesia (FSM). This is another American territory, and once again we were shocked by all the litter from American packaging. And we realized that the American villages lack the visual charm of most Pacific islands because many of the homes are made of debris—plywood and tin-- instead of natural materials like bamboo and palms.

There are five states within the Federation and we visited three of them.

On Ponape, a small unimportant island, we were amazed to find an extensive ruin made of stone built on a coral reef. We had never heard of this small city, Nan Madol, built with huge basalt "logs" as a political/religious/military center in 1200. Much of it is still standing. It can be accessed only by small boat or canoe.

Truk (now called Chuuk I'm surprised to find) is the largest lagoon in the world—40 miles across—and is the capital of the FSM. This became Japan's major military base in the Pacific during World War II, with seven airstrips in addition to the huge deep harbor. Since an American air attack in 1944, the harbor is now the repository of 250 Japanese aircraft and more than 50 ships. It's known as the biggest ship graveyard in the world and is naturally a top destination for scuba divers. Although neither Peter nor I scuba dived, we did snorkel on several of the shallowest sites so got an idea of the destruction.

We spent a lot of time on Truk because Peter came down with malaria while there. We had dutifully taken our malaria preventive pills when we were approaching or in infected areas but Peter had stopped taking his too soon. He was quite sick for a couple of weeks but luckily we well-prepared yachties had the cure medication on board and he recovered quickly.

Yap: Peter had been looking for traditional sailing canoes all over the Pacific but we hadn't found any so the tiny islands of Puluwat and Satawal were on our Must Visit list. They were the last of the islands where sailing canoes were still made and used.

Plus my step-cousin Sam Low had produced a film for PBS, "The Navigators", in which Satawal's chief navigator, Mau Piailug, was a principal player, so of course we had to meet him.

Mau was one of just a handful of men still alive whose knowledge of the sea and sailing routes in the entire Pacific had been passed down orally through generations. He had been recruited by the Polynesian Voyaging Society (PVS) to navigate the *Hokule'a*, a modern reconstruction of a double-hulled Hawaiian voyaging canoe, on its maiden voyage from Hawaii to Tahiti in 1976, using nothing but the sun, stars, winds, clouds, seas, swells, birds and fish to point the way.

My cousin, who is an anthropologist, a film maker and part Hawaiian, was aboard to film that successful journey, which provided evidence that ancient mariners had the knowledge to sail against the wind and currents, supporting the theory that the origin of Polynesians could be Asiatic and contradicting Thor Heyerdahl's conclusion that the Pacific had to be populated by South Americans on rafts like *Kon-Tiki*, carried northwest by those same winds and currents.

Peter's catamaran was a do-it-yourself boat designed by a Welshman named James Wharram. It was based on that very same double-hulled Hawaiian voyaging canoe recreated in *Hokule'a*.

Because of our large "double canoe," our welcome at Puluwat and Satawal was extraordinary. Peter was invited into the men-only huts where the hulls for their sailing canoes—nothing like ours-- were made from hollowed out breadfruit or mahogany trees, planks were sewed on with rope made from coconut fiber, and seams were caulked with breadfruit sap.

Each boat has one canoe hull and an outrigger. It's less than 30 feet long but a crew of six is required to sail it and they have to go long distances to find enough seafood to feed an island of 600 people every day.

Peter was invited to go for short sails on their proas but their main interest in us was our relatively huge (45 feet by 20 feet) double canoe's use as a fishing boat for them. We hosted a marathon fishing expedition for each island-- one was 36 hours-- sailing long distances to fertile fishing grounds. Each crew included several burly Micronesians clad in colorful loin cloths who toiled for many hours capturing everything from tiny fish to huge turtles.

Mau was among our Satawal crew but did not demonstrate his navigational knowledge for us. He and the other guys took turns at the helm, reading the compass.

But Mau's legacy lives on. He and the crew on *Hokulea's* maiden voyage are credited with sparking a cultural renaissance of voyaging, canoe building, and non-instrument navigation all across Polynesia, which is a huge segment of the vast Pacific Ocean.

Guam

In the northwestern Pacific cyclones are called typhoons. We spent the 1984 typhoon season plus a few more months in Guam, where Peter got a steady job in a machine shop. We anchored in a protected bay off a casual, friendly yacht club and near a creek where we went for shelter from several typhoon scares and one actual typhoon. We had only 80-knot gusts from Typhoon Bill. We were securely tied up to trees and had no damage.

Guam is another American Territory but unique in its Asian heritage. The indigenous people are Chamorros, the same as in the Philippines and Indonesia. First colonized by Spain for four centuries, it is thoroughly Roman Catholic. America got possession after the Spanish-American War. Japan occupied it during WWII but the U.S. got it back after that war. There are still large U.S. Navy and Air Force bases there, occupying about a quarter of the island, the largest in Micronesia.

Guam is now a major tourist destination for Asian countries and, interestingly, the Japanese are the main tourists. There were 20 large hotels when we were there, mostly on long beautiful beaches. We enjoyed many dinners in cheap but good Japanese restaurants.

I will be forever grateful for my time in Guam because it's there I got really interested in art. I lucked into free classes at the local university after meeting an artist who taught there. He lived on a boat at the Navy harbor across the bay but dinghied over to our yacht club many evenings for cocktail hour. When I asked him about art lessons I might be able to take while in Guam he invited me to audit his drawing classes. I drove our rattletrap pickup truck to the university three days a week for his classes, drawing all kinds of subjects in all kinds of mediums, and eventually graduated to figures.

I was hooked on figures. A homework assignment, a self-portrait in chalk pastels, was accomplished in the tiny cabin of our starboard hull, sitting on the head (toilet) to see myself in the miniscule mirror hanging over the small sink. I worked on it for hours, fascinated and thrilled that I could actually create a drawing that looked like me!

My final piece for that class was done in the classroom, a full figure of a young man in a straw hat relaxing on a lounge chair, drawn in black magic marker. I liked that one enough to bring it with me when I left the boat. It now hangs proudly in my bedroom.

Hong Kong

Another long passage, 16 days, from Guam to Hong Kong. We were going there mainly because Peter's family wanted to visit us there before we disappeared into the Indian Ocean. We passed by some of the Philippine Islands *en route* but didn't stop, as we had heard nothing but terrifying stories about pirates and thieves there. The South China Sea, famous for its rough weather, was kind to us. We had nice weather, making it slow going, but that was fine with me.

I had no idea that we would find green hills and uninhabited islands outside the city and was delighted when we found a marina in a suburban area. Rather than tying up to a dock, which we always tried to avoid, we were allowed to anchor out and use the facilities—showers, washing machine, mailing address-- for free.

The water was too dirty to swim in at that anchorage but it was far better than at the opulent, snooty yacht clubs in the city where elegant yachts are tied up cheek by jowl, along with multitudes of sampans and junks that live there, leaving just enough space for tons of garbage to float.

Peter's brother Bill arrived two days after we did it, so we explored new territory together. A couple of weeks later, Peter's father and niece Sandie arrived. Dad wanted to see mainland China. One day was enough for all of us, as we were required to be accompanied by a "guide" who never left our side. We went to Ghanzhou, formerly Canton, saw the sites and enjoyed a many-course meal. I apparently was most impressed by an ivory carving factory; in my journal I went on at great length about all the little people carving elaborate tableaux full of tiny exquisite detailed figures, using hand tools and electric dentist drills.

I was not a big fan of Hong Kong, except for the huge floating restaurants that were all terrific. I was turned off by the press of humanity everywhere you turned. Peter, surprisingly, liked it there. And another surprise, he had changed his mind about where we would go next. Instead of taking off for the Indian Ocean right away we would backtrack to the Philippines, then head west from there. This turned out to be a momentous decision for both of us and a very lucky one for me. I never knew why he changed his mind, why he decided he wanted to see the Philippines after all, but I was delighted that the Indian Ocean was postponed.

In all the years I spent on the boat I rarely questioned what I was doing or why. I was Peter's mate, doing what he was doing and, except for the occasional hairy interludes at sea, mostly loving it.

The cruising community was definitely a macho world. In almost every case the boats were owned and entirely operated by men. The women were there, like me, because their men were. Occasionally one would be known as "the awning maker" or a great baker but most of us had no identity to speak of except as the man's mate. I was "Peter's girlfriend" or "the *Solanderi* chick." My name meant nothing to anyone. I meant nothing to anyone. My past, my career, were unknown.

Once in a while I missed the recognition of my byline, but mostly I was content. I was living with the person I liked and loved more than anyone before or after. What more could I want?

But during the last few years I was on the boat I thought more and more about living ashore. The areas we sailed in were less and less appealing to me—the crime-ridden Philippines, over-crowded Hong Kong. The areas left to cruise through to complete the circumnavigation were downright terrifying. Piracy lurked in the Straits of Malacca and the entire Indian Ocean. And the thought of rounding the Cape of Good Hope, maybe the most dangerous passage in the world, absolutely petrified me.

So in the summer of 1985, when I left Hong Kong for my annual trip to the U.S. to see my mother in Connecticut, I made a side trip to St. Croix in the U.S. Virgin Islands. I knew the island only slightly but it had always beckoned to me: the beauty, the colors, the laid back atmosphere, the friendliness of the people, the open air restaurants and the jazz trickling out of the bars. And very important: It seemed to be a real place for real people, nothing artificial or touristy about it.

I arranged to spend a couple of days with my one acquaintance there, Tinker Bell Riggs, and asked her to set me up with a realtor, which she did. I thought I could buy a house and rent it out until Peter and I had finished sailing and were ready to move in.

I looked at available houses the first day and nothing appealed. So then I looked at building lots and was lucky enough to find the perfect spot: on a hillside in an undeveloped area with a beautiful view including ocean, a reef and a bay—a bay where we could moor the boat! And around the corner a marina and a boat-building business that specialized in multihulls – jobs for Peter!

Even though I knew virtually nothing about the neighborhood, or the island for that matter, and I certainly knew nothing about building a house, I bought the lot. It cost me $21,500. This was in 1985. Today (2019) it would be closer to $200,000.

When we back-tracked to the Philippines we cruised down the chain from Luzon to Cebu. I spent my spare time sketching floor plans. I was designing a house. I still intended to sail on with Peter but I couldn't get "my" island lot out of my head.

Then I found a lump on my breast, a large scary lump. A woman on another boat had recently had breast cancer surgery right there in Cebu and got me an appointment with her Chinese doctor. His office turned me off immediately—it seemed dirty and disheveled -- and when he told me I had cancer and should go upstairs to his operating room immediately I got out of there fast.

Back on the boat I realized this was my perfect excuse to back out of the impending voyage I dreaded. I would go "home" to Connecticut for surgery and the follow-up treatments, which could last for months. Peter should continue the circumnavigation without me. We had never made any commitments to each other. There was no discussion.

When I got to Connecticut and saw a surgeon there he informed me that my lump was a cyst. He lanced it and it went away. Of course I was terribly relieved not to have cancer. But I had made my decision. I was not going back. It was almost Christmas so I stayed with my mother for the holidays, then headed for St. Croix.

IV
MY HOME
St. Croix, U.S. Virgin Islands
1986-now

When I arrived on the island in January 1986 I was 53 years old and brought nothing with me but some salt-seasoned clothes, a floor plan and a bank account I hoped was big enough to build a house. Immediately I started to live a charmed life. My dear friend Tinker and her partner Leo let me live on their boat, *Tequila Sunrise*, and they introduced me to everyone they knew, especially those who might help me make my dream come true.

My friend Tinker Bell Riggs, who was my mentor in all things St. Croix.

Miraculously, by Christmas I was living in my very own dream house! My contractor, Barry Allaire, had pulled off an unheard of speedy building job.

I really lucked out. As I write this 33 years later, I'm sitting in the house I built on that lot I bought so recklessly and realize it is perfect. By dumb luck I have all the attributes I now know enough to look for. I'm in mid-island so can get to any destination within an hour. My house faces east so I get the prevailing breeze, which is almost constant, and rarely have to use my ceiling fans. I certainly don't need air conditioning!

I'm on a hillside, well above the dangers of a tsunami or storm surge or rising sea levels—and the sand flies or "no-see-ems". My house backs up to a cliff so that hurricane winds tend to blow up and over rather than into and through the house. Houses on the crest of a hill are too often blown to bits. Those on the beach can be washed away.

My house from behind shortly after it was built.

The house itself is small, 1300 square feet under cover. The floor plan is simple-- a 24-foot-square great room with a bedroom and bath on either side.

As a minimalist I furnished it sparsely so the small house feels plenty spacious, a quality I craved after living on a boat for 13 years.

Pastel houses are common in the tropics and I've painted mine pink.

Inside I've transitioned to a new favorite color—teal. My sofas and some of my walls now echo the blues and greens of the ocean. For several years even my refrigerator was teal. Appliances living near salt water are quick to rust so we have to paint our refrigerators often. Why not give it some pizazz!

As a first time homeowner, I had no idea what I needed. Barry had explained each step along the way and made many suggestions I thank him for every day. The washing machine and bathroom sinks and showers drain into flower gardens so that none of my precious cistern water is wasted. I don't like ceiling fixtures so he created indirect lighting in every room by simply hiding light bulbs behind a board where the ceiling meets the walls.

What makes this house special is the magnificent view and the long gallery (porch) overlooking the view. The gallery spans the front of the house—56 feet-- and is accessed through four sets of French doors flanked by louvered windows. These, by the way, are the only things on which I splurged. They are made from imbuia, a Brazilian walnut now protected—a rich dark wood.

My gallery, a 56-foot long outdoor living area overlooking a beautiful view. (The protective awning is not on the aluminum frame in this photo, which was taken in hurricane season.)
Photo by Diane Butler

At least some of these doors and windows are always open so that the tradewinds can blow through. The view and the breeze are so important to me I don't have screens. Thanks to my elevation and breeze, mosquitos are not often a problem, but I always have zap guns handy.

The view is beautiful, including a wide expanse of ocean, a coral reef protecting a big bay which shelters several boats, and green hills sparsely dotted with mostly unpretentious houses surrounding the bay.

The view that sold me on this spot and will keep me here forever.
Photo by Diane Butler

I'm on the north shore and on clear days can see St. Thomas and St. John, the other U.S. Virgin Islands, 40 miles away. On really clear days I can sometimes make out some of the British Virgin Islands, especially my old home Tortola, farther to the northeast.

I spend a lot of time sitting on the gallery just gazing at the view. I get up early, usually in time to watch the sunrise, which often is spectacular: pinks or peaches or even bright reds breaking through the clouds and then reflecting on the water of the bay.

Our clouds, by the way, are considered very special by every resident with whom I've ever happened to have a conversation on that subject. We seem to have a gorgeous display of every kind of cloud imaginable almost all the time. My favorite is the cumulus, the puffy white cotton ball clouds that most often fill our clear blue sky.

And our stars! We also claim that our stars are brighter and more plentiful than elsewhere. Without smog and tall buildings to block our view, and with little ambient light in a neighborhood like mine, the night sky is a clear black canvas generously sprinkled with shining stars.

The full moon, seen rising from my gallery, reflects a silvery glow off the gently rippling surface of the tranquil bay.

During the day the view changes by the minute —the blues and greens and fantastic turquoises of the water ebbing and flowing, the white foam breaking on the reef, sometimes gently, sometimes with gusto, small boats coming and going to fish or dive or sail.

It's a quiet neighborhood that has little traffic and lots of silence—which I appreciate more and more.

My surroundings have always played a big part in my state of mind. In my old age serenity has become my goal, and here I have it.

Through the doorway in my living room I see a few of my favorite things:
my dog Gus, my sculpture "Boy with Birds" and my view.
Photo by Diane Butler

Peter

Peter had come to St. Croix during my first summer, on his way to England to see his family. We had a great week or so sailing Tinker's boat to the BVI and seeing our old friends on Tortola. The ground had not yet been broken on my building site but the house plans had been approved. He especially liked that I had included a workshop for him.

But that's the last time I saw him.

When he left after that visit we both thought that he would continue sailing around the world for however long it took, then end up in St. Croix with me in "our" house. But the months went by and he was still in Cebu and communication got less and less frequent.

Eventually I learned that he was a father. Then a husband. Then again a father. It all happened so gradually that it didn't destroy me. I was building a new life for myself and I was happy. I felt I had made the right decision despite the outcome. I pitied him for falling into "the trap" he had always considered marriage to be, but I was happy for him when I learned he loved being a father! I never would have predicted that!

I'm grateful to have had that one great liaison that lasted for 13 years, longer than many marriages. I'm not sorry that I never had a husband; I'm self-centered enough to suspect I would not have made a good wife, and I always knew I didn't want children. I'm grateful that I was able to just fly away when I didn't want to do what Peter was doing anymore, and I'm grateful that Peter could just send me a letter to inform me of his marriage. I've always considered divorce a brutal process and am so glad I was never subjected to it.

My friends, hoping to console me, were sure that Peter was a victim of what was considered a typical ploy in that part of the world: the young Filipina, 20-30 years younger than the "rich European" (all white foreigners were called Europeans and were assumed to be rich) deliberately gets pregnant so the man would have to marry her and she would then have her ticket out of the Philippines.

They did move on to Hong Kong and Peter is still there, still living on a boat—a larger catamaran he built to accommodate his family. The little I know is that the marriage was bumpy and the wife was not around much, that Peter basically raised the girls himself. Both daughters are married now and one of the husbands is now helping Peter run the business that he "inherited" when his then boss retired! The business has something to do with boats, of course.

Salt River

My neighborhood is called Estate Salt River and my view includes the bay that connects the ocean to the estuary. In addition to its being the best "hurricane hole" for boats on the island, it also happens to be one of the most important areas of the island ecologically and historically, significant enough to have become a National Park a few years after I arrived.

The Salt River National Historical Park and Ecological Preserve, which embraces the entire bay and all the land immediately adjacent to it, was created in 1992 and I'm proud to say I was then an active member of the St. Croix Environmental Association, which was quite instrumental in bringing about the Park.

The land on the eastern point of the bay (I'm on the western point) was then threatened with the development of a large resort. Because the bay is so important ecologically, the environmentalists jumped in, creating enough hurdles to eventually force the hotel out and let the Park in.

Salt River's history goes back centuries. Rich in natural resources, it was occupied by a variety of pre-Columbian tribes. Petroglyphs from a Taino ceremonial ball park have been found on the western shore, in the same location Columbus later chose to visit when he "discovered" Saint Croix on his second voyage in 1493, the only landing he made on what is now American soil. He named the island Santa Cruz and claimed it for Spain, the first of the colonial "seven flags" that ruled the U.S. Virgin Islands until 1917, when the U.S. bought them from Denmark for $25 million.

The beach is now called Columbus Landing. It's a small beach fringed with palms and other trees, a pleasant part of my view.

The bay is ecologically important as the heart of the most complete web of life in the entire Caribbean, from wooded hills to river and bay, a mangrove forest, reef and submarine canyon.

I'm including a piece I wrote about Salt River in the early 1990s when I was asked to contribute to an environmental calendar by a woman in St. John who was putting together an ecologically themed VI calendar. The woman died soon after, so the calendar was never published.

I'm also including my poetry "suite" which was obviously inspired by that essay and in fact plagiarizes a few choice terms from it. That was submitted to *The Caribbean Writer* but also was never printed!

Salt River Eco Gem

Nature created a masterpiece at Salt River in St Croix—a tranquil bay with a complex of wildlife habitats unsurpassed in the Virgin Islands and probably the entire West Indies.

All the ecosystems of the tropics are represented in all their glory there on a uniquely uninterrupted continuum that flows in both directions, between uplands and abyssal depths.

Upstream the network is activated when it rains on Blue Mountain in the center of St. Croix. The water washes soil and nutrients down the slopes, across the riverbed and into the marine system through the best mangrove forest in the Virgin Islands.

Even Hurricane Hugo, which killed many of the trees, couldn't disrupt the food chain. The tangled roots of the mangroves continue to create nurseries for fish and other marine life and to filter out sediment and pollutants, allowing the natural nutrients of the bay to continue supporting fantastically diverse colonies of flora and fauna—on the muddy shores, in the sea grass beds and algae flats of the bay and out to the coral reefs, which in return protect the inlet from the ocean's full force.

Oysters and turtles, crabs and lobsters and all manner of fish thrive in Salt River. So does the most varied bird population in the Virgin Islands, including at least 11 endangered species. Most visible are the cattle egrets which commute daily to the island's pastures, flocking out at sunrise and returning as the sun sets. The mangroves also provide a seasonal haven for several migratory species such as warblers, the original "snow birds."

Salt River's perfect continuum carries on beyond the barrier reef to a remarkable submarine canyon where for several years the National Oceanic and Atmospheric Association operated an underwater habitat allowing marine scientists to conduct research for days or weeks at a time without having to come up for air. And beyond _that_ is the spectacular shelf-edge reef known to scuba divers as "The Wall". And finally the open sea.

There is a smattering of private homes on the hills overlooking the bay but otherwise the site looks much the same today as it did over 500 years ago, when Columbus anchored his fleet outside the reef on his second voyage and sent a boat ashore to look for fresh water.

Indians had discovered Salt River centuries before and several cultures had lived on the banks of this bountiful bay. One of them, the Tainos{?} had built a ceremonial ball park there. After Columbus, early European settlers focused their colonies there too and the Dutch built an earthen fort on the western headland. Evidence of both pre- and post-Columbian civilizations can still be found.

Today Salt River is the favorite "hurricane hole" for boats on St. Croix and a major center for dive boats and kayaks.

Developers wanted Salt River for resorts and marinas but, thanks to tenacious resistance by conservationists, the bay and its surrounding wetlands were finally saved in 1992 as the 916-acre Salt River National Historic Park and Ecological Preserve.

My essay for an environmental calendar

Salt River Suite

1. Bountiful Bay

Bountiful bay, calm and shallow,
a study in serenity.
Man comes and goes, you continue,
symbol of eternity.

Indians camped here prehistorically,
a primitive civilization.
Columbus found a native society
and commenced annihilation.

Then the colonists settled here,
they built a fort on the bay.
Seven flags fought for control,
you survived each fray.

Next a resort threatened to kill
the life that you sustain.
A National Park came to the rescue,
you can rest again.

Bountiful bay, Garden of Eden,
birds and fish abound.
Tranquil haven and habitat,
man can't get you down.

2. Historic Site

Columbus made one landing
on what's now U.S. soil.
On his second trip to the Caribbean,
he called at St. Croix.

The fleet anchored at Salt River Bay,
a long boat went ashore.
The sailors found an Indian village
and took two slaves or more.

The Caribs let some arrows fly,
the Spaniards fired some shot.
New World and Old were instant foes
on this historic spot.

3. Mangroves

A mangrove forest flourished here,
swampy, mysterious, green,
a jumbled thicket of tangled roots,
a jungle scene.

Today it is a graveyard
of ghostly silver limbs,
a monument to a hurricane
of 200-mile winds.

But nature's still at work here,
using the leggy roots
to hold back the sediment
that otherwise pollutes

and to shelter the wildlife
that survives here still
on the perfect food chain
even Hugo couldn't kill.

Dead mangroves harbor life,
now live ones can be seen,
seedlings shooting through the grey,
lovely and green.

4. Leatherback

A mammoth creature looms from the sea,
a prehistoric sight,
to lay her eggs where she was born
on a tropical beach at night.

She lumbers up the sandy strip
to nest instinctively.
The leatherback turtle picks a spot
and digs methodically.

Huge back flippers flick the sand,
three feet deep she digs.
She lowers her back end over the hole
and drops one hundred eggs.

They come in clusters, cue ball size,
until the very end.
Hiding the real ones with decoys,
ping pong balls she sends.

She fills the hole with sand again
and plods back to the sea,
returning several times a season
to leave more progeny.

Eight weeks later the nest erupts,
the hatchlings scurry out.
They make a dash for the water's edge,
there are predators about.

Only a few will live to renew
the cycle of fruition.
The huge and ancient leatherback turtle
is in danger of extinction.

5. Food Chain

Salt River is a textbook case,
a perfect demonstration
of Nature's extended family
and interdependent relations.

Birds and turtles, mangroves and grass,
coral reefs and sand,
all live symbiotically
where sea meets land.

Link by link the food chain passes
nourishment to and fro.
Animal, mineral, vegetable,
each contributes to the flow.

Baby fish and shell fish
get a sheltered start here,
Over a hundred bird types
spend the winter or the year.

Twenty seven threatened species
share the bountiful bay,
dependent on a food chain
that's still intact today.

A National Park will now protect
Salt River for posterity—
historic site and living lesson
in tropical ecology.

Making Money

Thanks to the Engelhard stock, which had been increasing in value over the 13 years I lived on the boat and spent very little of it, I was able to pay for my house without any loans. That was a total of about $158,000. (Today it would be around $400,000.)

But there wasn't much money left over so I needed to make some more. Tinker owned a storage company and I worked mornings in her office. I learned to use a computer and when her daughter Margot opened a shop full of Indonesian furniture and accessories I also worked for her a few hours a week and learned how to create a spreadsheet for her inventory.

I made another few dollars writing free-lance articles for the *Virgin Islands Daily News* and the *San Juan Star* Sunday Magazine, where my friend Connie was still the editor. Although I thought I would never write again when I quit working there in 1972, it was good to know I could still do it—and enjoy it!

Environmentalism

I became an avid environmentalist by chance. When I was living on Tinker's boat while building my house, a couple living on another boat in the marina were deeply involved in starting the island's first environmental group, SEA (St. Croix Environmental Association).

Fred Sladen and his wife encouraged me to come to meetings and I found I really cared about what they were doing. By the early 1990s I was helping in the office.

When the executive director, Robin Freeman, discovered I could write, she asked me to take over the newsletter, which I really enjoyed doing for the next nine years.

I also served on the board of directors—as secretary-- for three of those years. (I've always resisted board positions because I'm not a leader or an idea person and feel I have little to offer, but as newsletter editor it helped to be in "the loop.")

I'm proud that once during those years I was recognized by SEA as Environmentalist of the Year, an honor usually bestowed on activists. I have never been an activist so my contributions have always been behind the scenes, not upfront. I do not put myself "out there" because I'm extremely uncomfortable around conflict, contention or controversy.

Working with Robin opened my eyes to what it really means to be eco-conscious. She became my role model and Reduce, Reuse, Recycle is still my daily M.O., from composting my garbage to buying (almost) only used clothes.

There are many other very worthwhile non-profits on St. Croix, and I belong to and financially contribute to a lot of them. Up until recently I was often a volunteer. Once I turned 80 I decided I could retire.

Gardening

Thanks to a suggestion from my friend Tinker—one of many that were very helpful-- I volunteered at the nursery of our world-class botanical garden one morning a week. Up until recently called St. George Village Botanical Garden (named after the estate on which it's located), it recently changed its name to Botanical Garden of the Virgin Islands.

I knew nothing about tropical gardens. There I learned a lot and acquired the makings of a starter garden. I took whatever plants they couldn't use or sell at the nursery plus donations from the other volunteers' home gardens and planted them all around my property. It was a totally unplanned garden—and still is—but I like that. As long as I have lots of greenery and plenty of flowers I'm happy. And I like having other people connected to my garden. I still think of each donor almost every time I water this plant or cut that flower.

Me with Benji, my first dog on the island, planting ground cover.

I've hired a few different people to help me with the gardening over the years. With almost an acre of land, almost all planted, there's no way I can take care of it myself.

My helper for the last 20 years or so has been Edwin Cordero, who turned out to be a jack-of-all-trades as well as a gardener so now is absolutely indispensable.

He comes one afternoon a week for three hours and I have a long list of jobs for him every time. Often there is nothing about gardening on it but a potpourri of handyman chores that could include everything from plumbing or electricity to hanging pictures and changing light bulbs. Even computer problems!

I'm not the only single woman he works for so he's a very busy man but I know I can count on him to be here for me. I feel very lucky indeed to have such a talented and dedicated guy in my life. Every week it's obvious to me that I would not be able to stay in my house without his help. And staying in my house is top priority now. I wouldn't have a life without it.

Hurricanes

St. Croix has been hit by six major hurricanes in the 34 years I've lived here: Hugo, Marilyn, Georges, Lenny, Omar and most recently Maria. They are unquestionably the most negative factor in tropical living but have not succeeded in driving me out.

Every alternative location seems to have its own disaster potential: tornadoes, floods, forest fires, earthquakes. Chances of survival might be higher in hurricanes than any of those other catastrophes and, more importantly for me, they come with some warning, giving us time to prepare, physically and mentally.

There hadn't been a hurricane in St. Croix for 60 years when I was planning my house so they were not factored into my design. I did foresee the danger of a big overhang so instead of extending the house roof over the gallery I called for a separate "sacrificial" shed roof. It blew away in Hugo in 1989. I replaced it and that one blew away in Marilyn in 1995.

Since then I've had a large awning to cover my gallery instead of a hard roof. It's huge, but it can be taken down and stowed away if there is a threat of wind over 50 mph headed our way.

When I first got it I hired two or three men to wrestle it down for me. Once Edwin got involved he soon preferred to do it by himself. He's not a big guy but he's very strong and can manhandle that heavy vinyl cover by himself. Once we get it down, cleaned and dried and stowed away it's out of sight until hurricane season is officially over. There's no way we're going to go through that more than once a season. Hurricane season, by the way, is six months long—June 1 to November 30.

Hugo was a monster storm three years after I moved in. I was very lucky that my roof did not blow off but, like almost everyone else on the island, I had quite a lot of damage. The French doors and windows that open onto my gallery were blown away or badly damaged. I was able to replace them eventually and have since installed accordion shutters to protect them and clear panel shutters to cover smaller windows.

I have always gone elsewhere to ride out the actual storm; I and my dogs have imposed on friends who have an apartment or bunker under their homes. I feel safe under a foundation. But in case I ever have to stay in my own house, where I don't have such a luxury, I have created what I hope will be an adequate storm shelter in my guest bathroom by reinforcing the ceiling and door.

I do not consider leaving the island an option. I would not want to make anyone else feel responsible for my house and dogs.

And so far I've not been too traumatized by either a storm or its aftermath. For many the recovery period is what does them in. In the islands that's always long and doesn't seem to have improved a lot. After Hugo in 1989 I was without electricity for six months and after Maria, 30 years later, almost five months. But I had a generator that I ran for a few hours every day, solar lamps for evening, and access to ice to keep some food fresh. I drove to town every few days to find cell phone and internet signals. My needs are quite simple, and I had good training living on a boat.

Why don't I have solar panels and/or wind turbines? Coming from a boat where we were totally self-sufficient energy-wise, I intended to be off the grid ashore too. But in 1986 when I was planning my house, I was very discouraged to find that both were prohibitively expensive for me.

Swimming

I've always loved to swim and when I built a house a few minutes' walk from a nice beach I assumed I would be swimming there every day. Not so. Despite the reef protecting it from the ocean swells, the water off the beach is usually a bit choppy and I found myself with a mouthful of water every time I took a breath. That was a big disappointment.

The best swimming beaches on this island are on the western end, well protected from the prevailing easterly winds. That's too long a drive for a routine swim so I go there only for special occasions.

My mother was aware of my frustration and much to my surprise and delight offered to pay for a swimming pool. So a couple of years after I moved in, Barry and his crew were back on my site squeezing a 40x11-foot pool into the sheltered space between my house and my required setback. I named it The Kitty Pool in thanks to my mother.

I was never happy with the chlorine I had to use to keep the pool water clean so when salt-based purifiers came onto the market around 2012 I quickly switched over.

Kitty gets the afternoon sun so I'm usually in at the end of the day. I do only 20 or 30 laps now, ending with a nice long float on my back, the highlight of my day. I swim nude. As the water gently rocks my bare body, that's the closest I come to bliss. I also sleep nude when I have the house to myself.

Unfortunately my swimming season is only about six months of the year. I know it seems ridiculous to northerners who sweat even in our coolest months, but those of us who have been here long enough to have "thin blood" find the water too cold if the temperature dips to under 80.

Family Ties

One of the big benefits of settling on St. Croix was being within visiting distance of my family and friends. I was glad that they could see I had finally settled down—and in a place they were happy to visit!

My mother and her friend Ginny were my first guests, arriving just a few weeks after I moved in. I had furnished my house almost entirely from yard sales, from beds and sofa to pots and pans. Unable to find a dining table before their arrival I borrowed one from the local theater group, where I had been volunteering.

The morning of their arrival there were a few necessities still missing. It was a Saturday so I went to a yard sale and there found exactly what I needed: a bathroom mirror and a tea kettle!

My mother was able to return two more times before becoming bed-ridden. She loved everything about my new home, which made me feel good after all the years I had distressed her with my travels, especially the years at sea.

She died in 1995. I had the time and interest to clear out her house. It was such a nice experience I wrote this article about it.

My mother, who was 100% Irish, celebrating a birthday on St. Patrick's Day at my house.

Saying Goodbye

by Emy Thomas '55

After my mother's death, I volunteered to clear out her house. I wanted to be as close to her as I could. I wanted to say goodbye.

It was a sad, but surprisingly comforting, task. I had been warned it would be morbid and depressing, but I found it to be touching and sweet. Going through the treasures my mother had saved during ninety years, I learned a lot about her and liked what I learned.

My mother was Catherine McGeary '26, a redhead known as Kitty. She was a German major, active in Barnswallows, and a Tree Day Mistress who never enjoyed her moment of glory because the ceremony was rained out. She died in January 1995.

She loved her family excessively and was quite sentimental about us. She had saved every present ever given to her by a child or grandchild or great-grandchild, all the ugly dime-store knickknacks and tacky accessories. My mother, who prized good taste, had worn or displayed these gifts to please the giver for a while, then slipped them into trunks in the basement, where they remained for the rest of her life.

She died a fairly wealthy woman, but her most valued possessions, those in her safe-deposit box at the bank and her strongbox at home, included:

• the birth and/or marriage certificates of her parents, her husbands, and children;

• all of our baby teeth—my brother's and mine—cradled in cotton in an old wooden matchbox;

• a couple of "lucky" stones and a yellowed envelope containing some dried vegetation labeled Four Leaf Clover. (I remember her searching for them—my dignified mother down on her hands and knees earnestly, hopefully probing a clump of clover. I regarded her belief in lucky charms as one of her Irish traits.)

In the basement there were boxes and trunks full of letters. I was delighted to find love letters from both of her husbands. She had been widowed twice. I knew my stepfather had been crazy about her. I was twenty-five when they married and he told

Ninety Years of a Mother's Treasures

Catherine McGeary '26, MA'27

Emilia Thomas '55

Emy Thomas '55 is a free-lance writer who lives in St. Croix in the U.S. Virgin Islands.

everyone how he adored her, every day. But my father, who died when I was fifteen, had never displayed affection and I wondered.... When I dared to peek at the two letters she had saved from 1928, I was so relieved and pleased to read how he loved her, how much their approaching marriage meant to him.

She had saved every article I had ever published as a journalist and every letter I had ever written her. They were from boarding school and college and the cities where I had worked and the countries where I had traveled. I have brought them home with me, intending to read them some day. There might be a story there, although my letters to her never told the whole truth. Mum worried about me so much that I always felt I had to make her think my life was nearly perfect, that I was perfectly happy.

I opened one of my old letters at random while sitting on her basement floor and was sorry I had. In it, I apologized for behaving badly toward her on my last visit and having a bad attitude. For many years, I persisted in resenting her for what I perceived as interference in my life. Thank God I was finally able to forgive her honest mistakes, to realize she had done the best she knew how. Thank God I learned to say "I love you."

Among the many albums and boxes of photographs she had saved were several large and lovely pictures of her wedding to my father. My beautiful mother was serene and sylphlike in her flapper-length wedding dress. My father, with his hair parted in the middle, looked just like the Duke of Windsor.

While I sorted through her things, I found myself remarkably detached. I was pleased that I had time to take my time, to do a good job of it. I felt good about finding something special of hers to give to each of her special friends. I enjoyed spending time with her books, separating those that were appropriate for the country day school where she and my father had taught, giving the rest to the town library that she had loved and

A bead-and-glass necklace I had made for her when I was four was still in her jewelry box.

where, when her eyesight was failing, she had driven the staff crazy trying to keep her in large-print biographies. I felt her presence and her approval of my decisions.

Surprisingly, there was nothing left over for the Salvation Army or the church. Family and friends claimed everything, even the ball gowns she had danced in decades ago and the hospital bed in which she had died.

I filled six boxes for myself. There were clothes I could wear, household goods I could use, books and photos I wanted. There were things I had given her that I took back—cloisonné from Hong Kong, a hand-painted porcelain bell from Puerto Rico. I was gratified that she liked my presents; very few of my gifts had ended up in the basement trunk. A bead-and-glass necklace I had made for her when I was about four, fifty-eight years ago, was still in her jewelry box.

There were two things I didn't need or want that I felt compelled to take—my mother's old wooden sewing box and a brass-angel candleholder. They are not beautiful. As far as I know, they were not especially special to her. I know she loved angels, and this was one of several that came out every Christmas. The sewing box had been around all my life, but Mum herself hadn't sewn on a button in many years. Nevertheless, they are a part of her I felt I had to have.

The only possession that really distressed me was a hat—the straw boater she had worn when she visited me in the Virgin Islands before her final illness. She had looked like a little girl in that hat, so delighted, expectant, and vulnerable. I didn't want to keep it, I didn't want a memento that would break my heart, but I did want it to have a special home. I finally gave it to a friend of mine who was also a friend of hers.

Mum's house was empty then, and I had said goodbye.

An article I wrote after my mother died, as it was published in the Wellesley Alumnae Magazine, her alma mater and mine.

I'm sorry she was no longer around when I discovered a delightful connection between my past and present lives. An elderly acquaintance on the island, Ed York, had been a student of my father's at Romford, a boarding school for boys, in Washington, CT, in the early 1930s when I was a baby living on the campus! We discovered the link by chance in a casual conversation at a party.

Mr. Thomas had been his favorite teacher. Ed claimed he had been kicked out of every other prep school in New England before landing at Romford, where my father succeeded in straightening him out. Ed found old school photos including the two of them in their roles as baseball player and coach. This little discovery created a special bond between Ed and his wife Nina and me.

Another nice link was the discovery that a young cousin I knew nothing about had moved here shortly after the millennium. Megan Weary arrived when her husband, Rob, became director of the local office of The Nature Conservancy. Her grandfather John, my uncle, told her he thought I was living here. She looked up my name in the phone book at the TNC office and found it highlighted! I had done some volunteering there—a nice environmental connection. I enjoyed their company for the several years they were here.

My brother and sister-in-law, Tom and Joan, started visiting me after my mother died. This was wonderful because we finally had time to really get to know each other. All through our youth either he was away at school or I was away at school and our paths didn't cross much. Then I left home for good and he got married and started a family. When I made a visit to Connecticut I stayed with my mother in her new home and just stopped by Tom's for brief visits.

But when they were here for two weeks at a time we were almost always together and we finally got to really know-- and like-- each other. When traveling became too hard for them I started making two trips a year to see them and now we've really bonded.

White Hair

Some time around Hurricane Hugo, my hair turned all white. Not just the hair on my head but also the hair all over my body, including my eyebrows and eyelashes.

I had developed vitiligo, the condition in which the skin loses pigment in patches. I had always had a rather fair complexion but with my tropical tan the spots were quite unattractive so I consulted a dermatologist. He prescribed pills and sunbaths that didn't fix the problem so he changed my treatment to skin bleaching cream. I had started applying this to my worst areas, my chest and arms, when Hurricane Hugo interrupted.

That disrupted life entirely for months. I was too busy to think about how I looked.

When I realized later that all my spots were gone I also took in the fact that the hair on my head and all over my body had turned from dark to completely white.

Michael Jackson's transformation from black to white skin is well known, and presumably he and many others have used a bleaching cream similar to mine with similar results. But hair is never included in those make-over stories. And we've all heard how trauma can turn one's hair white overnight, but I don't think my switch was that sudden, and I don't think I was traumatized, and I don't know of any stories but mine in which hair all over the body transitioned from black to colorless.

It's a mystery I'll probably never solve.

First Book
Home is Where the Boat Is

Now and then an old acquaintance from my sailing days would find me on the island. Our memories of the cruising life and especially of Peter were delightful. I realized what a unique and interesting character he was—the quintessential "yachtie". That's what we on British boats called ourselves. Peter and his boat, *Solanderi*, were Brits.

We had occasionally run across cruisers who wrote up their adventures for yachting magazines. I had never had any interest in doing that but after these conversations I realized I could write a different story, one about the nitty-gritty of cruising around the world and the people like Peter and me who did it. It was a lifestyle most people knew nothing about.

It felt great to be writing again, and once I realized I was onto something that could become a book I started disciplining myself. I sat at my typewriter every morning until noon. If nothing happened I made myself stay there, writing something, anything, gibberish if necessary, until eventually something would click and I would be off.

Technology advanced as I wrote *Home Is Where the Boat Is*. I bought a word processor, the predecessor of the personal computer, during that period. What a blessing for a writer! To be able to delete without having to re-type! Ecstasy!

I ended up with a 146-page paperback book, covering everything you'd ever want to know about global cruising. With 36 chapters from Cooking to Survival. I spent about a year trying to get it published without success, then opted to self-publish. That was in 1993. It's still selling.

HOME IS WHERE
THE BOAT IS

Emy Thomas

The cover of my first book, *Home Is Where the Boat Is*

I dedicated the book to my mother, thinking she deserved a thank you for all the worry I had caused her. By the time it was published she was bed-ridden with assorted problems including painful osteoporosis, Crohn's disease and the beginnings of dementia. She was also nearly blind. But she, a former English teacher, was proud that I was an author and I very much wanted her to know how important my boat years were to me so I was thrilled that she wanted me to read the book to her. I was on a long visit and her attention span was short. I read a few pages a day. She loved it and I felt I had been forgiven for the distress I had caused her.

The book was well received in St. Croix and soon I was told of another good story: The first black man to sail singlehandedly around the world lived in St. Croix! An extraordinary man who should be quite famous and needed to have his story told!

Teddy Seymour, a modest St. Croix school teacher, made the circumnavigation on a 35-foot fiberglass sloop named *Love Song* in 1986-87. He was on such a tiny budget that he made only 12 stops and returned to St. Croix in a year and a half. He had no fanfare coming or going. He had a little press coverage in St. Croix but not much anywhere else.

I was certainly interested in that!

I met Teddy and we had a short conversation. A quiet and reticent guy, he didn't have much to say and he had no written material for me to read. But I hoped he might open up more and I was eager to write another book and I had just bought my first computer, a second-hand large and clunky machine, so I tried to start. I soon realized there was no way I, a white woman, would be able to "get into the head" of a black man and tell his story. Unfortunately no one else has written it either.

Alcohol

I was still drinking as I wrote that book, and I was aware that I wasn't as sharp after a drink as I was before, so my strict schedule included the prohibition of alcohol until I stopped writing at noon. Then I could bring out the wine.

I had wanted to stop drinking for many years. I knew I had a problem and almost every day I thought today is the day I'll stop, then gave into the urge once again. Finally I made it through one whole day, then another, and soon I felt pretty sure I was no longer addicted. I never felt tempted again.

Many former drunks remember the day if not the hour they had their last drink. I don't, but it must have coincided more or less with finishing that book in the early 1990s. I do know I never considered going to Alcoholics Anonymous meetings until about a year after that. I didn't feel I needed it; I wasn't having a problem staying sober. But eventually, after a terrifying trip home from a party with a drunk driver, I decided I needed new friends and went to a meeting the very next day. I was amazed to find I knew a few of the people there so immediately felt comfortable.

The meetings were great equalizers. In a population where blacks greatly outnumber whites, our AA meetings usually had more whites that blacks. Members were male and female, old and young, gay and straight, educated and illiterate, rich and poor, successful and homeless.

I attended meetings quite regularly for about a year. I was never completely comfortable there because of my phobia about public speaking-- we were sometimes called on to say something. Also, they ended each meeting by reciting the Lord's Prayer. I did not feel comfortable doing that and thought it was inappropriate for a non-church group. I understand a lot of AA groups have now dropped the practice, including the local one.

After a year or so I drifted away and never missed the meetings but I am very glad I put in that year because now I really understand and accept that I am an alcoholic, that I cannot have one drink. The transition was important; it merited some poems.

DRUNKPOEMS

A Celebration

On the sixth anniversary of my sobriety
I feel much less anxiety
and much more piety.
I've lost notoriety
but gained society.
I like the variety
found in sobriety.

Passing On

Paco has passed on.
He used to sprawl on the concrete stoop
of the burned out building
on the derelict corner of town
we call Times Square.

Hopeless helpless hapless Paco
A wretched loser
scooped up one morning
by street cleaners
with the broken and empty bottles.

I owe Paco.
His wasted, witless presence
scared me sober.
I pray that I can do for someone else
what Paco did for me.

DUI

Even when I drove off the road
and hit a tree and totaled the car
and had to have stitches next to my eye
I still didn't see that alcohol
had anything to do with it.

Now that I no longer drink
I see clearly I was DUI
and I'm horrified to understand how often
I blithely drove under the influence,
an oblivious instrument of death.

The Great Equalizer

As an anonymous alcoholic
I have a bond
with all the men and women,
black and white,
old and young,
rich and poor,
brilliant and stupid,
who share my disease.
Alcoholism is a Great Equalizer.

How It Happened

I drank to be sophisticated,
then to loosen up,
and then because I couldn't stop.

A group of poems I wrote after I stopped drinking.

Unitarian Universalist

AA had helped fill some sort of spiritual need for me. Before that, I realized, I had been worshipping alcohol; that's what I turned to in joy or sorrow. In AA my god was sobriety. Now I needed something else.

I had been introduced to the UU (Unitarian Universalist) Fellowship by a friend. I went to only one social gathering with him but learned enough to think that might be what I wanted now. It wasn't "religious" but it was a liberal's sort of spiritual place, promoting love, equality, social justice, inclusiveness and, importantly for me, environmentalism. They accept everyone including atheists and pagans. I went to one of their meetings and found there a few of the people I most respected. I joined.

I continue with UU for social and intellectual reasons more than anything else. I enjoy the company of like-minded people. Although I have tried to find a spiritual connection outside of religion, by meditating, yoga, tai chi or qi gong, or by reading Deepak Chopra and Eckhart Tolle etc., I cannot get there. I seem to have a mental block against the language and the concepts. I'm sure I'm missing something important, but I've made it this far without so I'm not going to worry about it.

Writers Circle

On a high after my first book was published, I knew I wanted to write more but didn't know what. My friend Roz also wanted to write so we started to meet once a week to read and discuss whatever we had written that week. This grew to a group of up to 10 people and is still going strong, now called the Writers' Circle. Writers of any kind are welcome.

I went through a period when poetry poured out of me. A big surprise because I've never been a big fan of poetry; I'm comfortable with plain homey Robert Frost but find most others pretentious or obscure.

Nevertheless, out it came. Some had humor, some a surprise twist. For a while it was all topical: drought, election, motor vehicle registration, litter. I seemed to have so much to write about I had the bright idea of offering my poems to the local newspaper, *The St. Croix Avis*. Here is the proposal I sent to the owner/editor/publisher:

Dear Rena Brodhurst,
We haven't met,
But I read your paper daily.
I'd like to suggest
A featurette
On island life in poetry.
Enclosed are some samples I'd like the Avis
To consider printing on a weekly basis.
Some poems are topical,
All are tropical,
Most will get a smile.
I call them Island Style.
Hoping you think the idea has promise,
I'm yours sincerely, Emy Thomas

I was disappointed that I got no response. In retrospect I wonder how I thought I could ever come up with a different subject every week!

Second Book
Life in the Left Lane

Eventually I started thinking about another book. I could write about island life from an expatriate's point of view. My treatment could be broken into categories—gardening, education etc-- as I had done successfully with the cruising life. And now I had a support group, the Writers' Circle.

I started writing. Every week I ran my latest by the group and digested the feedback. Eventually I settled on the title: *Life in the Left Lane*. There is a T-shirt company on the island that had trademarked this phrase but once I decided that was the title I had to have I spoke to the owner and got his permission to use it. Years later I realized I should have gotten that in writing, but there's never been a problem.

With both books I relied heavily on the comments of Connie Underhill, who had been my editor at the *San Juan Star* and whom I credited with making me a better writer. She had retired and moved to the states but I sent her each chapter as I finished it and she usually had suggestions that improved it.

This time I didn't even try to find a publisher; I knew my subject had a limited audience. Self-publishing and its ability to print-on-demand had become a big industry and there were several companies to choose from that did all the work for a reasonable cost. I chose Authorhouse and had *Home Is Where the Boat Is* re-published there too.

Life in the Left Lane was published in 2002. As I write it's 18 years old and still going strong. I re-read it now and then to see if I should attempt an update, but not that much has changed. What the newcomer needs to know about island time or making a living is still just about the same.

Local shops are the main retailers for both of my books and I am the distributor for them. Undercover, our only book store, has been a huge supporter, keeping close track of the stock and making sure they never run out of my books. My books are also sold on Amazon.

The cover of my second book

Until I started this memoir in 2018 I wrote nothing else for 16 years. I still felt like a writer and longed to be writing but didn't have another subject. There was nothing else I was that familiar with. Now and then I took a stab at fiction just so I could be working on something, but that never went far. I am a journalist, a writer of facts, and I just don't have the imagination or flair to make up a good story.

I had a brief moment when I got excited about writing a biography. I had visited the island of St. John, where Maho Bay Campground had made history as one of the first eco resorts. Its pioneer creator, Stanley Selengut, happened to be on site when I was there and agreed to be interviewed for an article in the SEA newsletter.

I was overwhelmed by his innovative achievements there—everything on the property was made from recycled materials—tires for floor tiles, newspapers for walls, etc; bread was baked in a solar oven; toilet waste was turned into compost. I thought he deserved a biography. I wrote him to suggest that I write one. He was nice enough to reply he thought it was too early in his career for a biography but thanks anyway.

A Painter

When I stopped writing, I started painting. I had been interested in painting for many years. I took some oil classes when I lived in Puerto Rico in the 60s and had occasional lessons when I lived on the boat but it wasn't until I settled in St. Croix that I really got into it.

I started with a watercolor class. My teacher arranged a small exhibit at the end of the term in which we all displayed some of our class work. I also wrote this poem, which became part of the show:

A LESSON IN WATERCOLORS

Choose a pretty subject,
draw it sketchily.
Watercolors are like a song
sung fast and joyfully.

Keep the composition simple,
eliminate a lot.
Zoom in on the focal point,
pull us to that spot.

Apply your pigments sparingly,
water them down.
Keep the colors soft and gentle
but don't let them drown.

Tilt the paper just a bit,
let the washes flow.
Leave a lot of white space,
the colors will glow.

Stop before you muddy them,
let the colors zing.
Strive for luminosity,
your painting will sing.

I also started a painting group with a few friends who liked to paint outdoors (*en plein air*). This eventually became known as The Palletteers and up until recently was still meeting weekly. It grew amazingly, up to 30 people some weeks in the winter when several snowbirds swelled our numbers.

We selected a different location each week, ranging from beaches and public parks to private homes. For several years we had our own art show at the Botanical Garden. I was amazed when on a couple of occasions my five or six watercolors sold out—and in a couple of cases I was asked to paint one of them again!

I segued into a minimalist phase, when I left a lot of white space and played with design. I called that My Chinese Period. My signature on those watercolors was made in what looked a bit like Chinese letters to me, placed vertically rather than horizontally on the paper.

Somewhere around the millennium I decided to try painting in oils. I liked the medium but couldn't take the smell of turpentine. A fellow Palletteer showed up for the winter with a new product: water-soluble oils. I tried them and loved them and immediately became an oil painter.

In the beginning I did a lot of scenes in my neighborhood—Salt River. It's definitely a picturesque area and I was amazed how many different features I found to paint: the beach, the boats, the marina, the endlessly changing interplay of sky and sea.

Eventually I started thinking of putting them all together as an art show. I knew I wasn't a great artist and was sure it would be considered presumptuous of me to suggest I have my own art show but I had encouragement and support from some top figures in the art world and so I went for it.

Serene Salt River

*Oil Paintings
by
Emy Thomas*

*Saturday & Sunday, March 1 & 2
Noon to 5 PM*

Columbus Cove
(the porch above the restaurant)
Salt River Marina
Route 80, North Shore Road

*The author of "Life in the Left Lane" and "Home Is Where the Boat Is"
(Books will be on sale)

The ad for my art show

On the funky deck above Columbus Cove, the restaurant at the Salt River Marina at that time, between 12 and 5 PM on Saturday and Sunday, March 1 and 2, 2008, about 200 friends, acquaintances and strangers signed my guest book, drank wine or beer, ate pretzels and popcorn and enjoyed the view of the boats and palm trees in the marina. By art show standards this was a very eccentric exhibit but it was perfect for me.

My subjects included the restaurant, the boats tied up to the seawall, the boats moored in the anchorage, palm trees and beaches, sun rises and moon rises reflecting in the bay, dinghies, kayaks, wind surfers, mangroves, surf, the multiple colors of the water and the visitors' center of the Salt River Bay National Historical Park and Ecological Preserve. I sold most of them and I also took the opportunity to sell some books.

Sally and Hugh, the proprietors of the restaurant at that time, didn't charge me for the space, and I went home $4400 richer. (My prices ranged from $200 to $500.) It was definitely the best party I ever had.

Me at my art show, with six of the 20 paintings shown.

I continued painting in oils for years, was a founding member of the Artists Guild of St. Croix, showed in several exhibits and had greeting cards made from some of my images, which are also sold at Undercover and some other shops.

Three of my paintings that were made into greeting cards, from left: Red Carpet (watercolor from "My Chinese Period"), Pot Party and East End Scene (oils).

A couple of years ago, when I was about 83, I started to lose my touch. Suddenly I couldn't mix the colors I wanted, I couldn't apply the paint to the canvas smoothly, I couldn't lighten the darks or darken the lights satisfactorily.

I still have a closet full of painting supplies and am not ready to toss it all out quite yet, but I'm not really expecting a resurgence of talent-- or even interest.

Art Museum

One of St. Croix' most unexpected surprises is a beautiful art museum. The Caribbean Museum Center for the Arts (CMCArts) is a handsomely restored building on Strand Street in Frederiksted which hosts a number of exhibits every year featuring artists from all over the region. It is also a hub for nurturing creativity in children.

It is the brainchild of Candia Atwater, a lawyer who settled here shortly after I did and very soon saw a need which she determined to fill. She filed non-profit articles of incorporation, for which I was a signer, and started producing exhibits of local artists' work at various locations on St. Croix. In 1995 she started publishing what became an annual calendar full of paintings by regional artists: Island Art & Soul. I was happy to be the editor of that for most of the first 25 editions.

Candia's perseverance paid off when a benefactor finally showed up and the dream became a bricks-and-mortar reality in 2005. It is a major asset to the island's cultural scene.

My Art Collection

The first painting I ever bought was in Tortola, when I was living on the boat. A man on another boat in Maya Cove was an accomplished watercolorist and I loved his work so much I bought a painting of shacks and palm trees on Salt Island, one of the sparsely settled small islands in the BVIs. I think I paid him $75 for that and somehow managed to find a space on the boat where I could hang it.

When my house was finished and I realized I had a lot of blank walls, I embarked on an art collecting journey that's still going on 34 years later. My walls-- and a closet-- are now full of art work by St. Croix artists, all of whom I know personally and some of whom are good friends. My "collection" is based solely on what appeals to me, not on monetary value, but they are the only possessions I have mentioned in my will.

My only really valuable art piece is a small (about two feet tall) copy of a large sculpture by the late San Juan-based artist Lindsay Daen. "Boy with Birds" is outside, the centerpiece of my view. He's surrounded by tropical vegetation against a background of turquoise bay, foaming white reef, wide sapphire ocean and endless cerulean sky adorned with ever-changing fluffy white clouds. (See photos on back cover and pages 87 and 88.)

Travels

When I first settled on land after years of sailing, I was sure I was travelled out. But great trips kept presenting themselves and since I've been living in St Croix I've traveled to Kenya for a photo safari, Costa Rica on a birding expedition, Machu Pichu and an Amazon boat trip in Peru, an art tour in Eastern Europe, a conference in Cuba when it was still "closed" and a tour of the Northwest US, including the San Juan Islands.

My trips to the mainland were mostly to see family and friends in the northeast but I also had a memorable RV tour with friends Queenie and Tinker to the Four Corners in the southwest. There I was so enamored of the many National Parks we saw I resolved to see many more, but 22 years later I have yet to begin.

One annual event I try not to miss is a reunion with my San Juan friends. I lived there only six years (1966-72) but still feel very close to a small group of gringos, all of whom moved back to the states since then and get together every summer, first at one's country home in Pennsylvania and now at another's lake house in New Jersey. We are still great friends.

A group of friends I made when living in Puerto Rico in the 60s, all of whom now live in the northeast US and meet yearly for a reunion. This was the gathering in 2008. Two who are mentioned in this book are Connie Underhill, my editor, upper left, and Deirdre Cooper, my first visitor on the *Green*, the other woman in back row. I'm in green shirt.

Animals

I have always had at least one dog since I've been in my own home. A total of 11 in 33 years. All rescues, all lovable. For a single woman living alone, a dog or two is a fabulous companion. I can't imagine living without at least one.

I've had up to three at a time. They've ranged from poodle mixes to German Shepherd mixes, from whirlwinds to couch potatoes, from one who wouldn't voluntarily come into the house to one who rarely came out from under the bed. Somehow they each had a huge place in my heart.

We have deplorably large populations of abandoned animals in the islands and a wonderful organization, the St. Croix Animal Welfare Center, doing amazing work to save those critters. Since our population of animal lovers is not big enough to take them all in, many of our animals are sent to the states, where our Crucian mutts find welcoming homes.

I've escorted a couple of animals north and arranged for house guests to do the same and I've also fostered a few dogs until they found adopters.

My most successful foster case was Madeline, a cute little Chihuahua mix. My niece Kathy and three of her children were visiting then and the kids instantly fell in love with the dog and hounded their mother to adopt her. Kathy was not interested as she already had three cats and many rabbits to take care of but at the last minute she capitulated and signed adoption papers. Maddie is now the queen of Kathy's home and "the best thing that ever happened to" her.

Many rescued dogs come with names given them by the animal shelter staff or the individual rescuer and often I'm not wild about the name. In the beginning I renamed my adoptees, but when a friend pointed out "that's the only thing they come with" I quickly started acting on her thoughtful suggestion.

Thus I've had a Sarah, a Pearl, a Franny and a Phoebe. I almost had a Manzanilla and a Klaus but fortunately one of our most dedicated dog rescuers, Donna Cascarelli, got to them first and changed their names to Cupcake and Gus while fostering them back to health and before passing them on to me. Gus had been found sick and starving by the side of the road on Christmas day, hence Klaus. Cupcake was simply Donna's must name for that adorable small and fluffy white puppy. At first I was reluctant to have a dog named Cupcake—a bit TOO sweet—but I grew to love it; it was certainly better than the Spanish word for chamomile.

Gus is the only dog I have now, a shaggy-haired blond Terrier mix who is the easiest, least needy dog I've ever had. He's content to just hang out wherever I am. He is so laid-back it's no problem if I'm late with his dinner or skip a morning walk. If he could talk he'd probably say "Whatever."

Gus, my current companion.

His positive personality helped him deal with a horrendous attack by three neighborhood Rottweilers. We were on our usual morning walk when they assaulted him. Neither the stones I threw at them nor my shouting deterred them, and they seemed determined to pull Gus apart. Luckily my nephew John and his kids Jen and Brian were visiting me. I screamed their names over and over until they woke up and ran—barefoot on a rocky dirt road--quite a distance to the scene of the crime and saved us.

Gus recovered from his many wounds and has never shown any fear of those dogs, which we can see from my house. I, on the other hand, have PTSD about the incident and have had to cut back my neighborhood walking considerably as I can walk only in the opposite direction now.

Other animal life around my property includes iguanas (one of whom drowned in my pool and another which lives on the roof of a shed and poops on my pool deck), the occasional deer, an ever-decreasing population of birds and butterflies, and two special creatures with whom I'm familiar enough to have named.

Blue is a small blue heron that hangs out on the road leading to my driveway, mostly at night. There are flocks of them roosting in the nearby mangroves but why he chooses to walk alone on a pot-holed dirt road in the dark is a mystery. He started young, when he was still all white. I got to see the blue feathers take over one by one. (A few days after I wrote this paragraph I found a perfect blue-grey feather right there. I took it as a thank you for including him in my book!)

Liz is the equally original name of the little lizard that visits me at lunch time most days. I assume it's a she because she's sweet and gentle, pretty and graceful. She's important, a St. Croix *anole*, an endemic species. She comes up on the table top while I'm eating lunch on the gallery and actually eats crumbs from my hand. These lizards are similar to geckos and are welcome inside the house, where they hang out on the walls and eat any mosquitos passing by.

Reading and Puzzles

Books, crossword puzzles and jigsaw puzzles are my other companions. When I need a break from whatever I'm doing I often turn to a crossword or jigsaw puzzle. They clear my mind. But when I have a block of time I can devote to reading that is my favorite thing to do.

Fiction is my favorite genre and I'm reading more and more as I'm doing less and less outside. If it's a well-written book, I'll probably like it, which means I'm into mostly "literary fiction", as opposed to genres like mystery, fantasy or science fiction.

Thanks to the wonderful local bookshop, Undercover, plus friends with whom I swap and the local thrift shops, which have excellently organized book sections, I'm discovering many new-to-me writers that I love, mostly women. I'm also reading and re-reading lots of classics.

And a few years ago, after the University of the Virgin Islands held its first literary festival in many years, a small group of us was so enraptured by the Caribbean literature we were introduced to we agreed we had to read much more. We started CaribLit, a monthly book club, in 2015, and it's still going strong. Our little area of the world has produced many exceptional writers who have written marvelous stories set in the islands' past and present.

Friends

Now that I'm really old, most of my contemporaries have disappeared from the island. Most of them are fellow statesiders who settled on St. Croix to enjoy their golden years in leisure, warmth and beauty.

But then something changed. They found they are more attached to their grandchildren than they ever expected and want to be part of their early years. Or they are spooked by a hurricane, or crime. Or, most often, they develop a health issue that can't be handled here. Many of them have returned to the states, often reluctantly, for that reason alone. There are still a few left and we usually try to get together for holiday meals and birthdays. I call this group the SOLOS—Single Old Ladies Only.

I have been very fortunate to acquire new and younger friends in recent years, many of them in their 60s. They have certainly brightened up my life! Most special are Laurie Ingersoll and Apple Gidley, both of whom arrived on the island several years ago and were introduced to me soon after thanks to the common interests of writing and painting.

Laurie is a writer and illustrator of children's books and Apple is a writer of historical fiction. They met each other through the Writers Circle, which they each learned about from me. We have become a threesome. If I had any maternal qualities I might think of them as surrogate daughters. But since I don't, I just feel honored-- overwhelmed really-- that they have sort of adopted me.

Apple lives just 20 minutes away and I enjoy her company often. She has made it clear that I am to count on her for any need, including medical advocacy; I am so comfortable with her that I'm sure I will do that if ever necessary. Laurie moved to Florida a few years ago but stays in close touch, making sure I'm pampered on birthdays and other occasions.

These two fabulous women teamed up to give me a fabulous treat in May of 2019: a road trip with them from Winterpark, FL, where Laurie lives, to Houston, TX, where Apple and her husband John still have another home. We were celebrating the end of a bad year for me, one with two surgeries and three hospitalizations. Emy's Epic Escapade was 18 days full of learning and laughter. A nice reminder what fun "girl friends" can be,

Apple, Laurie and me on cover of book Laurie put together commemorating our Epic Escapade.

Health

St. Croix has a dubious reputation for health care but I have always felt that it's good enough for me, that I don't want to live to be 100 anyway. I've been lucky to be strong and healthy well into my 80s and, until recently, when others catalogued their aches and pains in what my friend Roz calls "organ recitals", I would proudly pipe up: "there's nothing wrong with me."

I have regretted that boast since August 7, 2018, when I was visiting family in Connecticut and stomach pains sent me to The Hospital of Central Connecticut, about a mile from my brother's house, the very same hospital, then called New Britain General, where I spent a stressful summer working when I was 16.

On this re-visit at age 84 I was whisked from the emergency room into surgery for a perforated diverticulitis (a hole in my colon). As I understand it there is no way to predict or prevent such an event.

My recovery was interrupted twice by obstructions caused by scar tissue, which were removed in both cases by a tube down my nose to my gut through which bile was gradually removed. The first time I was still in the Connecticut hospital, where I became a bit of a celebrity during my 23-day stay as the little old lady from the exotic island of St. Croix who walked multiple laps around the surgical floor several times a day. Two months later, after I had returned to St. Croix, a second obstruction sent me to the local Juan F. Luis Hospital. It's never been considered quite up to par, but I'm happy to say I had a good experience, that despite the hospital's major damage from Hurricane Maria, everyone performed well.

The worst part of this saga was the colostomy that was part of my first surgery. I coped poorly with that. Although I had long intended to never again step foot in the north in the winter, I braved New England in February because that was the soonest I could have the colostomy "reversed". It was another major surgery but I recovered easily, in plenty of time to enjoy my Escapade.

After both surgeries I had excellent places to recuperate. Much as I love my brother I find his household stressful so I was grateful to have offers of the quiet homes of my niece Kathy, who lives five minutes from my brother's house, and my friends Sue and Bob Filene in Cambridge, Mass. Both were excellent retreats with great cooks helping me back to normal.

I'm now in good health. I don't look good, because I'm covered with wrinkles, age spots and other skin imperfections, and I'm all hunched up because I have both osteoporosis and scoliosis but, remarkably, though I hesitate to boast again, I have no pain or disability.

Now I hope to stay that way and simply enjoy the rest of my life, however long that is, in my ideal home. I hope that when the time comes I will be lucky enough to simply die in my sleep. If I'm unlucky enough to reach the point where I can't take care of myself, I'm quite sure I will not want to live any longer. There will probably be a most unlikely end to this most unlikely story.